Filmguide to

La Passion de Jeanne d'Arc

INDIANA UNIVERSITY PRESS FILMGUIDE SERIES
Harry Geduld and Ronald Gottesman,
General Editors

Filmguide to

La Passion
de Jeanne d'Arc

DAVID BORDWELL

INDIANA UNIVERSITY PRESS
Bloomington London

Published in Canada by Fitzhenry & Whiteside Limited, Don Mills, Ontario
Library of Congress catalog card number: 72–88634
ISBN: 0–253–39301–9 cl.   0–253–39302–7 pa.
Manufactured in the United States of America

contents

preface

In preparing this volume, I have been indebted to several people: Mary Corliss and Charles Silver of the Museum of Modern Art Film Study Center who helped obtain scarce documents and made the Museum's print of *Jeanne d'Arc* available; Dorothy Desmond of Audio-Brandon Films who loaned me the Gaumont print for study; Destin LeBlanc who patiently translated important German material; and Kathryn Kane and Mark Johnson who proofread late into the night. As ever, I am grateful to my wife Barbara for her acute editorial advice.

Filmguide to

La Passion de Jeanne d'Arc

credits

LA PASSION DE JEANNE D'ARC

(Original title: La Passion et la Mort de Jeanne d'Arc)
Société Générale des Films, 1926–1928.

Screenplay	Joseph Delteil and Carl Theodor Dreyer
Direction	Carl Theodor Dreyer
Photography	Rudolf Maté, assisted by Barth Kotula
Editing	Carl Theodor Dreyer
Art Direction	Hermann Warm and Jean Hugo
Costumes	Valentine Hugo
Historical Consultant	Pierre Champion

Time: 110 minutes.

Filmed from May to October 1927 in Paris. Premieres: 21 April 1928, Paladsteatret, Copenhagen; late April 1928, Paris; 28 March 1929, Little Carnegie Playhouse, New York.

CAST

Jeanne d'Arc	Renée Falconetti
Bishop Pierre Cauchon	Eugène Silvain
Nicholas Loyseleur	Maurice Schutz
Jean Lemaître	Michel Simon
Massieu	Antonin Artaud
Jean Beaupère	Ravez
Jean d'Estivet	André Berley
Guillaume Evrard	Jean d'Yd
Other judges	Jean Hemm, André Lurville, Jacques Arma, Alexandre Mihalesco, Robert Narlay, Henri Mallard, Jean Aymé, Léon Larive, Paul Jorge, Henri Gaultier

In 1952, a sound edition of the film was produced by Gaumont-Actualité and supervised by Lo Duca. Musical accompaniment was taken from works of Scarlatti, Albinoni, Gemianani, Vivaldi, and Bach.

outline
La Passion de Jeanne d'Arc

1. COURT OF ROUEN CASTLE

Hands turn pages of old book. Judges assemble to try Jeanne under the eyes of the English army. Presiding Judge Cauchon reads charges. Jeanne is brought in, her feet chained. English general Warwick enters to observe proceedings. Jeanne is interrogated about her past: she weeps at the memory of her mother. Jeanne says she was born to save France and that the English will soon be driven out. A soldier shouts at her threateningly. Questions about Jeanne's vision of St. Michael. To what purpose does she wear men's clothes? "The salvation of my soul!" Jean d'Estivet shouts and spits at her. De Houppeville announces that the girl is a saint and falls to his knees. Soldiers march him out. Protests from judges. Jeanne asks to be taken to Pope. Judges assert by vote that they are qualified to judge her. Has God promised Jeanne salvation? Jeanne says yes, but she knows "neither the day nor the hour." In anger, Cauchon adjourns the session.

2. JEANNE'S CELL

Clergy plotting to trick Jeanne crosscut with Jeanne seeing shadow of cross on cell floor and braiding crown of straw. Loyseleur and Cauchon supervise the forging of letter supposedly from King Charles. Jeanne attacked by soldier, who takes her ring. Loyseleur intervenes. Jeanne trusts forged message and Loyseleur. Cauchon watches through peephole. Further interrogation: Did God promise to release her from prison? Is she sure of being saved? Loyseleur encourages her to answer yes. "Are you in a state of grace?" Loyseleur will not help her. She answers: "If I am, may God keep me there; if I am not, may God put me there." Priests retire, baffled. Guards mock Jeanne with her crown of straw and a mock-scepter. Massieu comforts her.

3. TORTURE CHAMBER

Subjective shot from Jeanne's point of view as she enters. Judges tell Jeanne that Satan has deceived her and demand that she sign the recantation. She refuses. Torture machines set in motion. Quick montage of spiked wheel. "Even if you separate my soul from my body, I will revoke nothing." Pace of machine's turning and sequence's cutting increases. Jeanne faints and is taken back to cell.

4. JEANNE'S CELL

Massieu oversees preparation of Jeanne's bed; her crown is tossed aside. Crosscut doctor's bleeding of Jeanne with conspiracy of Cauchon, Warwick, and Loyseleur. Jeanne awakes; Cauchon is at her bedside. She asks for her body to be buried in holy ground. Communion brought into her cell. Priest holds up wafer; recantation pushed toward her. Jeanne refuses to sign. Communion withdrawn; Cauchon berates her and refuses to let her hear mass. Judges, furious, stalk out to summon English executioner.

5. CEMETERY

Judges go outside, where crowd has gathered; soldiers oversee. Jeanne brought out on stretcher. Sermon exhorting Jeanne to recant or be burned. Tracking shot to executioner on his wagon. Jeanne looks from rotting skull on grave to flowers growing nearby. Massieu and others urge her to sign; Loyseleur says she must still fight for her country. Jeanne signs recantation. Cauchon reads verdict: life imprisonment. Crowd cheers; Warwick rages. Soldiers throw scuffling bystander into pool of water.

6. JEANNE'S CELL

Close-up: bits of hair fall to the stone floor. Jeanne's hair is cut, penitent- and prisoner-fashion. Crosscut with townspeople attending a fair. Jeanne's hair and crown of straw swept out as trash. Frantically, Jeanne summons judges and retracts recantation: "I renounced God to save my life!" Does she believe she is God's messenger? She nods, condemning herself. Judges are sorrowful. While communion is prepared, Massieu asks wherein lies her victory. "It will be my martyrdom." And her deliverance? "Death!" Crosscut communion procession with preparation of stake. Jeanne is given communion as Loyseleur watches. Crosscut communion with townspeople rushing into Rouen Castle and soldiers preparing to control the crowd.

7. CASTLE COURTYARD

Jeanne led out to the stake. An old woman gives her a drink. Crowd watches as Jeanne presses a cross to her bosom. Crosscut baby at mother's breast. Executioner binds her to stake. When rope slips off, she hands it back to him. Massieu holds up crucifix. The wood is ignited; Jeanne is burned. She screams: "Jesus!" Crowd and even some soldiers are driven to weep. "You have burned a saint!" Warwick orders his soldiers to attack the crowd. Swift montage of the struggle. Soldiers' maces lash into women and children. Cannon is fired into crowd. People slowly beaten back across moat as drawbridge is raised. Close-up: the flaming stake and a cross in the distance.

the director

A Holy Seriousness

Five hundred years after an illiterate peasant girl died at the stake, she continues to haunt our lives. Generally ignored before 1800, officially commemorated by Napoleon, and sporadically celebrated in the nineteenth century, Jeanne d'Arc has become a living presence in the art of our time. Her story has been dramatized by Shaw, Brecht, Anouilh, Claudel, and Maxwell Anderson, set to music by Honegger, Dello Joio, Jolivet, and Paray, choreographed by Martha Graham, and filmed by Méliès, Rossellini, Otto Preminger, Victor Fleming, Bresson, and Dreyer. As we would expect, such diverse modern artists have interpreted Jeanne's story from various, highly personal angles. Compare, for example, Anatole France's Jeanne, a hardy country girl, with Shaw's extraordinarily sophisticated soldier-heretic. In opposition to Mark Twain's pious maid (what Shaw called "an unimpeachable American school teacher in armour"[1]) stands Brecht's grotesquely parodied evangelist, Joan Dark, who comes to learn that saintly suffering is foolish and only violence will change the world. Likewise, Ingrid Bergman's passionate, vital heroine in Rossellini's *Giovanna d'Arco al rogo* seems a world away from Florence Carrey's ascetic, numb victim in Bresson's *Procès de Jeanne d'Arc*. In the light of such diversity, it is not surprising that Carl Dreyer's film *La Passion de Jeanne d'Arc* strikes us as absolutely unique. Like most artists drawn to Jeanne, Dreyer has taken what interested him, using her story to help define his own recurring artistic preoccupations. In the process, he has created one of the most significant and beautiful works in film history and one of the noblest Jeannes in our century's art.

In early 1922, after Dreyer had already directed four films, he admiringly described Benjamin Christensen, another Danish director, famous for his *Witchcraft Through the Ages* (1921), as "a man who knew exactly what he wanted and who pursued his goal with rigor and tenacity, never becoming discouraged by any sort of difficulty."[2] For Dreyer, Christensen was "a man of ideals, who did his work with a sort of holy seriousness."[3] However apt this judgment may be of Christensen, it perfectly fits Dreyer himself. Throughout a career spanning fifty years, Dreyer clung to his individuality in the face of indifference and discouragement. Only such zeal could, for example, have secured his independence during the silent era. Between 1918 and 1928, he made nine films, shot variously in Denmark, Sweden, Germany, Norway, and France. This output includes a formula melodrama (*The President,* 1920), a historical allegory (*Leaves from Satan's Book,* 1921), a sprawling historical narrative (*Love One Another,* 1922), a fairy tale (*Once Upon a Time,* 1922), a lyrical romance (*The Bride of Glomdal,* 1926), two intimate chamber dramas (*Mikael,* 1924, and *The Master of the House,* 1925), and two films that resist easy classification (*The Parson's Widow,* 1920, and *La Passion de Jeanne d'Arc,* 1928). Some of these were personal projects, others were commercial assignments, but all bear the stamp of an individual creative talent. Dreyer freely admitted his debts to Griffith, Stiller, and Sjöström, and the styles of German expressionism and *kammerspiel* also affected him, but his work eludes the neat boundaries of influences and movements. In each film, Dreyer's idiosyncratic vision overrides the contingencies of nationality and studio demands; the independence of will he admired in Christensen is present from the start of his own directorial career.

After the silent period, Dreyer's tenacity was put to a still more severe test. The legal wrangling following *La Passion de Jeanne d'Arc* and the fiasco of the independently-made *Vampyr* (1932) made him an exile from filmmaking. It was not until 1943 that he managed to shoot another feature, *Day of Wrath.*

After *Two People* (1945), a marginal work, and some minor documentary filming, another long silence ensued, broken by *Ordet* (1955). And after almost ten more years, there appeared *Gertrud* (1964). In short, of Dreyer's fifty years of commitment to filmmaking, half were spent outside film production.

Only Dreyer's integrity and force of will sustained him during these decades of inactivity. Although cinema was what he called "my only great passion,"[4] he refused to make films on any terms but his own: he turned down an invitation from Hollywood because he disliked the script and declined a directing job in Nazi Germany because of the government's anti-Semitism.[5] Not that these years of involuntary retirement were completely sterile: while writing newspaper articles in the 1930s and managing a theatre in the 1950s, Dreyer was constantly planning projects. More often than not, though, the projects were never realized. His *Maria Stuart,* his *Light in August,* and his *Medea* (envisaged for Maria Callas, long before Pasolini's version) interested no producers. The bitterest failure of all was that of his *Jesus* film, a project which he conceived in 1948. The conviction that he would one day make this film sustained Dreyer over twenty years of painstaking research and dashed hopes. Finally, when he was seventy-eight, the Italian television corporation RAI offered to finance *Jesus.* It was too late. Dreyer died three months later.

The same "holy seriousness" that ruled Dreyer's entire career dominated the making of each film. Again, his model was Christensen, whom he saw as "a man who did not *fabricate* his films but who *created* them with love, choosing every detail."[6] Even before he broke free of studio regulation, Dreyer sought total control: while making *Leaves from Satan's Book,* for instance, he chose the subject, cast nearly all the parts, wrote the script, and designed the settings. Later in his life, he argued vehemently that the director must always write his own script ("Allowing

others to prepare a scenario for a director is like giving a finished drawing to a painter and asking him to put in colors"⁷)
and must exhaustively research his subject (Dreyer compiled his
material, one collaborator recalled, "as if in preparation for
a thesis"⁸). Likewise, Dreyer dominated his casts, tirelessly rehearsing his actors in order to extract precisely what he wanted;
stories still circulate about how, while filming *Day of Wrath,* he
kept an old actress bound to tall poles for hours in the blazing
sun. Dreyer's relentless will must have often made him a difficult
man, but the films that resulted have a purity, a density, and a
controlled beauty that may have been unachievable any other
way.

Dreyer's seriousness was "holy" in a double sense: not only
did he treat his work almost as a sacred calling, but his art itself
sought the spiritual. Regardless of locale or time, a Dreyer film
is almost invariably about powers beyond ourselves: the cyclical
power of nature (*The Parson's Widow, The Bride of Glomdal*),
the remorseless powers of time (*The President*) and fate
(*Gertrud*), the awesome power of death (*Vampyr*), the ambiguous power of love (*Love One Another, Mikael, The Master of
the House, Day of Wrath, Ordet*), and the affirmative power of
grace (*La Passion de Jeanne d'Arc*). Dreyer's recurring
subjects—communal intolerance, martyrdom, witchcraft, miracles, and sainthood—are metaphors for the confinement of the
spirit by earthly restraints and the liberation of the spirit by insight into unearthly powers.

Again and again, Dreyer presents the intersection of this
world with another, the impinging of the eternal upon the everyday. Satan's reappearance in each episode of *Leaves From
Satan's Book,* for instance, situates the heroine's final self-sacrifice within a timeless perspective. In *Day of Wrath,* Anne's love
has supernatural undertones, giving her the power to summon
her lover and kill her husband. And in *Vampyr,* David Gray walks
from a normal twilight into a nightfall of dread and damnation.

Sometimes Dreyer's protagonists accept the spiritual dimension of life as an eternal cycle: in *The Parson's Widow,* the lovers and old Dame Margaret realize their place in the rhythm of nature, and in *Ordet,* faith in the miraculous power of this rhythm redeems a wasteland of hatred and despair. But sometimes too, Dreyer's protagonists choose to renounce totally the everyday in order to seek the eternal. The old artist in *Mikael* forgives the betrayal by the youth he loves and dies with an image of ideal beauty and love before him. In both *Day of Wrath* and *Gertrud,* the protagonist discovers that the love she seeks is not to be found on earth and resigns herself to solitary suffering. For Dreyer, this is no pious passivity; the world his tragic protagonists leave always has possibilities for some happiness. But what he finds supremely intolerable is any confinement of the individual, any denial of one's integrity. So the individual struggles. In the less sombre films, love overcomes oppression, and peace is established. But when Dreyer's heroine is forbidden to define herself by reference to her spiritual ideal, she must reject this world altogether. Like Dreyer himself, his tragic protagonists assert their integrity by repudiating easy compromise and by committing themselves to spiritual values.

But how can one make what seems a steadfastly concrete medium like the cinema reveal such spirituality? By stylistic and formal abstraction. "Abstraction," Dreyer wrote, "allows the director to get outside the fence with which naturalism has surrounded his medium. It allows his films to be not merely visual but spiritual."[9] First, he argued, the director must *simplify.* The process of concentration, stripping down, intensification, is basic to Dreyer's work. His scripts, usually adapted from plays, radically compress time and space: a few days and a few locales (*Day of Wrath, Gertrud*), a single night in one area (*Vampyr*), two days in one basic locale (*Ordet, The Master of the House*), two hours in one apartment (*Two People*). Likewise, the text is pared down to the absolute minimum—little local color or flamboyant dialogue and almost no subplots. "In the cinema," Dreyer remarked, "the words are very quickly relegated to a background which absorbs them, and that is why you may retain only what words are absolutely necessary. The essential is sufficient."[10] Similarly, where von Sternberg wraps his actors in a cocoon of veils and smoke, Dreyer purifies his sets starkly. While making *Ordet,* for example, Dreyer had his crew fill a set with the normal equipment of a rural kitchen, then he systematically removed objects one by one until he had reduced the decor to a few basic elements. The same principle controls the films' rhythm: regardless of whether Dreyer uses very short shots (an average of one every five seconds in *Jeanne d'Arc*) or very lengthy shots (one every minute and a half in *Gertrud*), he rarely complicates his films with the elaborate tempi of Renoir or Truffaut. Amédée Ayfre puts it well:

> The temporal rhythm of Dreyer's films is not that active and practical rhythm of everyday life. The minutes which pass are not those of the chronometer or the speaking clock [of the Paris Observatory]. Here is a time of the soul which seems to have undergone a great magnification. . . . A bit of time is set apart from History, stretched out, enlarged, and brought before us in the present.[11]

In Dreyer's world, no action is casual, so each must be carefully scrutinized; like Mizoguchi, Dreyer suggests that if the camera gazes at the action long enough, the essential will prove sufficient.

Such simplification pushes the film sharply toward abstraction and prepares for the second stage of the process: symbolism. Dreyer's mise-en-scène gives objects and characters symbolic overtones by their isolation and position. When, for example, Gertrud advances toward the lover of her youth, he sees her in the mirror that connotes his devotion and her vanity. The death of Zoret in *Mikael* occurs midway between a crucifix and a statue of a naked youth; the composition diagrams both the aesthetic and spiritual dimensions of Zoret's love. Certain images—crosses, birds, clocks, sheep, candles—recur emblematically throughout Dreyer's work. Above all, there is the mysteriously powerful symbol of light—the light that floods over an erotic painting in *Mikael,* that eventually rises over the murky landscape of *Vampyr,* that ignites Anne's eyes in *Day of Wrath,* that envelops the characters at the close of *Ordet* and *Gertrud,* that bursts out of almost every frame of *Jeanne d'Arc.* Light, combined with Dreyer's characteristic slow rhythm, gives the action a certain grandeur, an unearthly monumentality; but also it can signify a spiritual clarity, an acknowledgment of a radiant order beyond normal experience. In such ways, simplification and symbolism give Dreyer's style a timeless autonomy which is admirably suited for suggesting the spirituality his principal characters seek.

As a result of Dreyer's intense force of will, his rigorous control of every artistic element, and his unique forms, styles, and themes, his films have a contemplative density—their own "holy seriousness"—which makes few concessions to what Hollywood vacuously calls "entertainment values." "The public," Dreyer once confessed, "never enters my thoughts for a moment."[12] Dreyer's films can horrify, puzzle, sometimes amuse, and nearly always exalt the spectator, but they do so on their own terms. Like their creator and many of their protagonists, the films are uncompromising, but, if responded to openly and without prejudice, they can afford us rich and unique experiences. To the study of one such uncompromising yet rich film, *La Passion de Jeanne d'Arc,* the rest of this book is devoted.

the production
Living Jeanne's Drama

Perhaps only in the Paris of the late 1920s could Carl Dreyer's vision of Jeanne d'Arc have taken exactly the form it did.[1] Between 1926 and 1928, Paris teemed with avant-garde experiments and antics. At this time the Surrealists were gathering force: their official gallery, opened in 1926, was exhibiting works by Ray and Tanguy; a few Surrealists had successfully disrupted the opening of the Ballet Russe's *Romeo et Juliette;* Breton had published his first major essay on the "Surrealist Object"; Man Ray was working on his film *Emak Bakia,* and Buñuel and Dali were preparing their film *Un Chien Andalou.* Experiments in music encompassed the radical classicism of Stravinsky's *Oedipus Rex* and *Apollon Musagetes,* the pulsating rhythms of Honegger's *Rugby* and Ravel's *Bolero,* and the Satie-like simplicity of Milhaud's *Le Pauvre Matelot.* In the theatre, Louis Jouvet, Charles Dullin, the Pitoeffs, and Gaston Baty were assaulting the Naturalism of the previous generation; Jean Cocteau was writing plays as diverse as *Orphée* and *Antigone;* and at the Alfred Jarry Theatre, Antonin Artaud was shocking audiences with *Burned Stomach, or The Mad Mother* and a production of Claudel's *Break of Noon* that ended with Artaud's stepping onstage to denounce the author as a traitor. In the commercial cinema, Marcel L'Herbier, Germaine Dulac, and Jean Epstein continued to work as exiles from Impressionism, but the outstanding commercial film of the time was Abel Gance's highly experimental *Napoleon,* which burst upon Paris in triple-screen fury in 1927. Appropriately, amid all this avant-garde activity, Dreyer was for once given complete autonomy ("I had a free hand, I did absolutely what I wanted"[2]) and he was permitted to experiment as never be-

13

fore. Moreover, he drew many of his collaborators from the artistic world of contemporary Paris, so that by the time *La Passion de Jeanne d'Arc* was finished, the production had yielded not only a great film but an extraordinary example of how artists can cooperate when coordinated by a single powerful creative vision.

That vision was ruled by one fiercely enforced principle: intensity at all costs. Dreyer's intensification at every stage, from scripting through shooting to editing, made the film a collaborative enterprise of an unprecedented kind: his compelling energy and holy seriousness resurrected enough of Jeanne's spirit to make the cast and crew feel that they were participating in something unique, magic, even sacred.

Dreyer—like Bernard Shaw—had become interested in Jeanne after her canonization in 1920, so that when the Parisian success of his *Master of the House* prompted the Société Générale des Films to offer him a contract, Jeanne was one of the subjects he proposed. (Dreyer later claimed that the choice among Jeanne, Marie Antoinette, and Catherine de Medici was made by drawing straws![3]) The producers proceeded to buy the rights to Joseph Delteil's sentimental biography *La Vie de Jeanne d'Arc* (1925). In early 1927, Delteil published a quasi screenplay[4] and when the film was finished, he shared screenplay credit with Dreyer, but Delteil's actual part in the production was slight. Dreyer discarded Delteil's script and wrote his own, based on Pierre Champion's authoritative edition of the trial text. (Champion later became the historical consultant for the film.) Dreyer's script compressed the several months of Jeanne's trial into a single day—a daring experiment in unity and the first step toward the intensity which he would seek at every stage of production.

When Dreyer began preparing the film in 1926, he decided that it would be a talking picture. But he discovered that as yet European studios were not equipped for sound and *Jeanne d'Arc* would have to be shot silent. Nevertheless, his script retained a great deal of dialogue which, contrary to standard silent film procedure, the actors were to speak *in toto. Jeanne's* numerous dialogue titles were later to become a bone of critical contention, but Dreyer insisted on focusing on the intimate spoken drama.

Unlike technological developments, casting was totally under Dreyer's control. Some players were passers-by recruited from streets and bistros; the English general Warwick, for example, was played by a café-keeper. Other parts were filled by professionals of the most diverse sorts. Eugène Silvain, then in his seventies, had a lifetime of performances at the Comédie Française behind him when he was selected for the role of Bishop Cauchon. Michel Simon, who took a small part, was a successful stage actor and would later become famous in films by Renoir and Vigo. Antonin Artaud, current *enfant terrible* of avant-garde theatre and the Marat of Gance's *Napoleon,* took the role of the sympathetic Brother Massieu. But whether nonactor or professional, each player was chosen by one principle: how well could he or she incarnate the essence of the character? The question became especially acute when Dreyer considered who was to play his heroine. Lillian Gish was discussed as a possibility, but Dreyer was drawn to a young Comédie Française actress, Renée Jeanne Falconetti. After seeing her in a light comedy, he called on her at her apartment. "It was a beautiful woman with a coquettish smile who sat facing me. Her makeup was perfect—in itself a work of art."[5] But Dreyer saw a different woman underneath: "Behind that makeup, the pose, behind that modern and ravishing appearance, there was something. There was a soul behind that facade."[6] As she took off her makeup for screen tests, she protested that she looked ugly, but Dreyer knew Falconetti was his Jeanne.

Dreyer's technical collaborators were likewise carefully selected, representing a range of international avant-garde talent that fully justifies Léon Moussinac's calling *Jeanne* a "Franco-German-Danish film."[7] The Polish cameraman Rudolf Maté had assisted Karl Freund on several UFA films, notably Dreyer's own

Mikael (1924). From France came the costumier Valentine Hugo, then allied with the Surrealists, and her husband Jean Hugo, whose stylized decors for *Romeo et Juliette* (1924) had made him one of the leading young stage designers of the day. Hermann Warm, who collaborated with Hugo on sets, had worked in the cinema since 1912 and had masterfully designed such classic German films as *The Cabinet of Dr. Caligari, Die Spinnen, Der Müde Tod,* and *The Student of Prague.* If for nothing else, *La Passion de Jeanne d'Arc* would be memorable for having assembled one of the most artistically prestigious casts and crews of any film in history.

These heterogeneous talents were able to blend into a unified whole by virtue of Dreyer's rigorous insistence on intensity. As he had stripped Falconetti of her makeup, so he eliminated the trappings of the conventional period-film. Historical accuracy of dress was respected up to a point, but, as Marcel Martin has noted, the costumes are "para-realist"—derived from a period but stylized enough to give them "a timeless simplicity."[8] Similarly, Dreyer insisted that the decor be spare, bright, uncluttered—in short, abstract. Arches and columns were designed as neutrally as possible, while the crookedness of windows and distant houses was inspired by medieval miniatures. Such intensification, simplification, and stylization were, as always for Dreyer, steps toward the expression of spirituality. "I sacrificed embellishments," he wrote, "for the sake of truth."[9]

After eight months of preparation, shooting began in May 1927. Now Dreyer's absolute will became most demanding. Anticipating a long period of filming, he had shrewdly cut costs by renting a Billancourt auto factory as a studio and using the equipment of an adjoining film company. Given sufficient time, his strategy was to involve the entire cast and crew in the film as profoundly as possible. Among his collaborators he built up an extraordinary intimacy. During shooting, Warm, Maté, and Dreyer took rooms together and constantly discussed production:

"We lived only for this film," Warm recalled.[10] At a still deeper
level, Dreyer plunged the cast and crew into Jeanne's story itself
by shooting the film in chronological order. Although this created some technical problems (Warm had to design portable sets
that would quickly slide away on overhead tracks), the psychological pressures were much more critical. Valentine Hugo
watched the tension of the story invade the cast:

> We submitted to this oppressive atmosphere of terror, of an
> iniquitous trial, of an eternal judicial mistake, all the time. . . .
> I saw the most cautious actors, carried away by the will of the
> director, continue to play their roles unconsciously after film-
> ing. For example, after a scene in which a judge appeared
> touched by Jeanne's sadness, he muttered, "At bottom, she was
> a witch!"—living this drama as if it were real. Likewise, an-
> other judge, foaming with rage, running out of invective, shot at
> the accused a reprimand smacking of court-martial: "You are
> a disgrace to the army!"[11]

Thus Dreyer's holy seriousness, intensified in the script, charac-
terizations, decors, and costumes, infected the entire production
as, day by day, scene by scene, Jeanne's death drew near. "We
were not making a film," an assistant director recalled, "we were
living Jeanne's drama, and we often wanted to intervene to save
her."[12]

Dreyer had other ways of driving the cast and crew to live
Jeanne's drama. All items of makeup, even wigs and false whisk-
ers, were forbidden, so that actors confronted each other as men,
not as masks. Falconetti's hairdo was so short that she had to wear
a wig off the set, while actors playing judges and priests shaved
their heads in Dominican fashion. (Dreyer recalled with amuse-
ment that Artaud had a hard time explaining his tonsure to his
Surrealist friends.[13]) Moreover, Dreyer ordered sets that would
make the players feel as if they were living in them. Warm con-
structed a miniature town, complete with gate, moat, drawbridge,
surrounding walls, watch towers, and main street. The producers

were outraged to learn that in the finished film this expensive set was never seen in its entirety, but it admirably served Dreyer's purpose of giving his players a tangible sense of milieu. Dreyer's will power elicited a comparable dedication from the camera crew, who dug deep holes around the set for low-angle filming and built a hanging camera stand to get upside-down overhead crowd shots. Even the extras were caught up in Dreyer's zeal as he drove them to weep frantically at Jeanne's immolation.

But above all Dreyer's energy focused on Falconetti, the heart of the film. In the living Jeanne's drama, she underwent great physical and psychological hardships—kneeling on stone floors for hours, contorting her body in awkward positions, submitting to the shouts and spit and torture of her accusers; only the bloodletting scene was performed by another actress. Dreyer worked her relentlessly, playing scenes over and over, with screens set up around her or with all personnel banished from the set. He and Falconetti would study the previous day's rushes in search of what Dreyer called "some little fragments, some little light that rendered the exact expression, the tonality we had been looking for,"[14] and they would begin again from there. Indeed, so intense were Dreyer's demands that some have accused him of immersing Falconetti *too* deeply in her role, of torturing her no less cruelly than the judges tortured Jeanne. It is hard to see how else Dreyer could have elicited from an actress celebrated for light comedies a performance of unequaled tragic power. As Dreyer himself wrote, "There is no greater experience in a studio than to witness the expression of a sensitive face under the mysterious power of inspiration. To see it animated from the inside, and turning into poetry."[15] That this inspiration did come from the inside, not from any threats or bullying, is evident not only from the performance itself but from the fact that as shooting continued, Falconetti gradually took complete command of her role. She needed no rehearsal by the time the cast arrived at the climax of both the production and Jeanne's drama.

Valentine Hugo has left the most vivid account of the final days of shooting. Here the production's intensity and intimacy, the crew's profound identification with both heroine and actress, Falconetti's incredible dedication, and Dreyer's compelling energy and humility culminated in one of the most memorable moments in film history.

> In the silence of an operating room, in the pale light of the morning of the execution, Dreyer had Falconetti's head shaved. Although we had lost old prejudices [against short hair on women], we were as moved as if the infamous mark were being made there, in reality. The electricians and technicians held their breaths and their eyes filled with tears. Falconetti wept real tears. Then the director slowly approached her, gathered up some of her tears in his fingers, and carried them to his lips.[16]

The living of Jeanne's drama could hardly go further.

Filming ended in October 1927, and, after several months of editing, *La Passion de Jeanne d'Arc* was premiered in Copenhagen on April 21, 1928. When it opened in Paris at the end of the same month, a controversy arose about church censorship of the film. At the script stage, the Archbishop of Paris had objected only to the scene in which a priest tempts Jeanne with communion. (Dreyer nevertheless included the scene just as he had planned.)[17] Upon the film's release, though, the Archbishop demanded many excisions. Léon Moussinac sarcastically reports that without Dreyer's permission, the distributors complied with the Church by "reducing the interest of *La Passion de Jeanne d'Arc* to a historical episode, and history revised and corrected for church youth clubs at that."[18] Whether any uncut versions were shown in Paris is difficult to say, but when the film finally reached the United States, it was evidently complete.[19] Its reception in Britain was more hostile; because of its alleged "anti-British" attitude, the film was banned for at least a year.

In subsequent decades, copies of *La Passion de Jeanne d'Arc* survived only by luck. The film was drastically recut and given a sound commentary in the United States in 1933. Despite the film's popularity in cinema clubs, in 1936 one of the original negatives could be bought in London for only £ 80. By the end of the war, all negatives were believed lost in a laboratory fire, but in 1951 a negative was found and given to the Cinémathèque Française. From this excellent print Lo Duca made a sound version for Gaumont, adding new titles and music. (He claimed that Dreyer approved the use of Bach, Vivaldi, and Albinoni as accompaniment, but Dreyer later maintained that the film's rhythm was completely destroyed in the sound version.) Today the Cinémathèque (silent) version can be found in archives like the Museum of Modern Art and George Eastman House, while the Gaumont sonorization is the one most commonly in commercial distribution.

What became of the participants in the production? Rudolf Maté and Hermann Warm collaborated with Dreyer again on *Vampyr*. The Hugos and most of the actors returned to stage and film work, while Artaud went on to formulate a theory of a "theatre of cruelty." Although it was announced in 1929 that Dreyer and Renée Falconetti were preparing a new film, *Catacombs,* she too returned to the stage, eventually bought her own theatre, and played Jeanne on stage in 1934. During the war she fled to Switzerland, Brazil, and finally Buenos Aires, where she died in 1946.

There are inconsistent reports of how *La Passion de Jeanne d'Arc* fared commercially, but its high budget (seven million francs, as compared to the average production cost of half a million), surely contributed to the difficulties of the Société Générale des Films. Founded to supply money for artistic films, the Société supported some outstanding efforts—*Jeanne,* Gance's *Napoleon,* and Epstein's *Finis Terrae*—until the coming of sound and the decline of independent French production in the late twenties threw the company upon hard times. Dreyer's contract was broken, he sued, and in the autumn of 1931, he won damages. It was the court case and its entanglements which persuaded Dreyer to seek independent financing for *Vampyr*.

Regardless of *Jeanne*'s financial career, the production remained an indelible experience for the participants. Calling the project "a marvelous apprenticeship in so many things I have never seen in the cinema before," Valentine Hugo remembered Dreyer as a man "who knew what he sought and got it."[20] "I regard my work with Dreyer," said Artaud, "as one of my unforgettable memories."[21] And Hermann Warm, after fifty years of distinguished work in the cinema, still maintains that *Jeanne d'Arc* is his best effort.

But Dreyer was equally grateful to his collaborators, particularly to the woman who had sacrificed so much in order to live Jeanne's drama. He later recalled that on the day when Falconetti's hair was cut, "everyone, even the technicians, had remembered to bring her flowers. But not me."[22] Doubtless his gesture on the set was a fair substitute, but the gratitude he felt lingered for almost forty years. In 1964, he completed his last film, *Gertrud,* the story of a woman who dedicates herself to an ideal love. Why did he select Paris for the film's premiere? To leave a bouquet, he explained, on Falconetti's tomb.[23]

5 ·
analysis
The Triumph of the Soul Over Life

The intensity Dreyer sought during the production of *La Passion de Jeanne d'Arc* is visibly and emotionally present in the film itself. But this very intensity, at once painful, exultant, and mysterious, may not seem to invite critical analysis. One's response to such an overpowering film tends to be resolutely private; hence, perhaps, the tendency of most critics to discuss the film in vague and confessional terms. Yet as an organic work of art, *La Passion de Jeanne d'Arc* repays study. If we examine what is going on visually, dramatically, and thematically in the film, our experience can be the richer for it.

The film's power, I believe, proceeds in large part from its tension between concreteness and abstraction. The unforgettable faces, the tactility of the objects, and the immediacy of the action yield an impression of vivid specificity. At the same time, Dreyer strives to transcend the concreteness of his images by means of an abstract form and style. By compression and stylization, the film charges reality with a unique significance. *La Passion de Jeanne d'Arc* perfectly illustrates Dreyer's dictum that "Abstraction allows the director to get outside the fence with which naturalism has surrounded his medium. It allows his films to be not merely visual but spiritual."[1]

This abstraction begins with Dreyer's radical transformation of the story of the historical Jeanne. Unlike Shaw, Dreyer ignores Jeanne's military and political accomplishments and focuses entirely on her trial and execution. From the questions and testimony Dreyer takes nearly all the film's dialogue, but he alters the time scheme drastically: the five months and twenty-nine sessions of Jeanne's trial are in the film concentrated into

one day and five interrogations. Many of the issues in the trial—
Jeanne's alleged witchcraft, the magical powers of her ring, the
question of her virginity—are eliminated from the film, so that
Dreyer focuses on the principal charge leveled against her: that
her persistent belief in the sanctity of her visions and the holiness of her mission constituted a refusal to submit to the authority of the Church. In addition to the religious issue, Dreyer emphasizes the historical fact that Jeanne's trial was a political one,
carried out by the clergy but rigged by the English.[2] Yet even
the historical elements that enter the film become significant only
as they affect Jeanne's fate: the film's conflict of the spiritual and
the political doesn't aim at interpreting history but at defining
the struggle within the heroine. On the whole, the narrative's
elimination of much historical background and its spatial and
temporal concentration represent the film's tendency to move
away from the concrete circumstances toward an abstract time
and space.

At the stylistic level, we can see the tension as one between
the shot as *reality* and the shot as *image*. What is the fence with
which naturalism has surrounded cinema? It is, in one sense, the
cinema's power to denote reality: the reality of a time–space
continuum, of a world evoked beyond the edges of the screen,
of movement-in-depth which suggests three dimensions. What,
then, is abstraction but an emphasis on the shot as *image,* as the
destruction of the time–space continuum, the construction of
the shot as a closed world, and the creation of a schematic flat-
ness—of, in short, a tendency to free the image from denotation.
One mark of a film's visual style will thus be the way it accom-
modates itself to the inevitable tension between the shot as reality (representation) and the shot as image (abstraction). In *La
Passion de Jeanne d'Arc,* Dreyer's shots are pushed toward the
abstract pole, but never so far that they lose concrete reference.
A unique dialectic of specificity and generality, of concrete and
abstract, informs Dreyer's visual style.

Take, for example, the typical content of the shots. Certainly details of setting (a door, a window, a stool) are sometimes shown, but to this concreteness is opposed the neutral white walls and sky framing the action. Directors like Rossellini and Von Stroheim, who are interested in history as history, would begrime the walls and surround the characters with a clutter of everyday objects of the period. But Dreyer, who uses history to bracket and distance the action, makes the spatial arrangement of actors and objects highly symbolic. The priests dominate Jeanne by towering over her; the latent violence of the soldiers is conveyed by the spears jutting up around Jeanne's head; a cluster of judges, closed as tight as a fist, expresses their conspiracy. Likewise, the flat, unshadowed lighting which bathes almost every shot in the film emphasizes the image *as* image. Thus although the images are concrete in reference, the decor, compositions, and lighting tend to lift the narrative out of its historical context into an abstract time and space—what Siegfried Kracauer aptly calls "a no-man's land which is neither the past nor the present."[3] These walls are at once of the Middle Ages and outside time; these judges are at once historical personages and personifications of the variety of evil; this is both Rouen prison in 1431 and an abstract sign of Prison itself.

Functioning inseparably with the neutral decor and lighting and the expressive compositions are the film's close-ups. Many viewers erroneously remember *Jeanne d'Arc* as a film composed entirely of close-ups, and it is evident where this misconception comes from: although the camera is frequently at a great distance from the characters, one gets a *sense* of close-up, even in the long shots, because the spare decor and plain costumes force our attention to the characters' faces, and the lighting sharply brings out their expressions. With the film's genuine close-ups, we are again confronted by a dialectic of representation and abstraction. On one hand, the people we see, all devoid of make-up, seem utterly natural: "a documentary of faces," Bazin calls the film.[4] On the other hand, the very principle of the close-up—eliminating the inessential and magnifying the essential—is an *abstracting* one. The close-up, Jean Mitry writes,

> gives a tactile, sensuous impression of things. But in isolating things, it makes them a kind of symbol: the object becomes the living representation of the concept which it figures forth, an *analog* for a pure state of mind. One can then say that the close-up is even more abstract on the intellectual plane than it is sensuous on the perceptual plane. Nothing is more concrete than what the close-up shows, but nothing is more abstract than what it suggests.[5]

In *Jeanne d'Arc* this abstraction of the close-up is assisted by the pure decor and lighting and the stylized costumes and compositions so that, isolated in a frame, almost detached from a real setting, the film's concrete actions, objects, and faces are pushed toward the status of pure signs. Shots of Jeanne's arm being twisted by a guard, of a cynical priest picking his ear, of torture spikes, of a skull, of the cross, of Jeanne herself, symbolize ideas and psychological states.

It is in the juxtaposition of these close-ups that the dialectic of concrete and abstract is most fully developed. Dreyer's use of narrative time and space is crucial here. While each shot embodies a concrete, real duration, the cutting constantly compresses time: when a priest bows at Jeanne's feet, we see only the final phase of his movement; when a soldier rushes to Jeanne, the entire duration of his crossing the room is collapsed into two shots—one of him rising and another of him beside Jeanne. Interestingly, only in the quick montage of the torture machines does Dreyer notably *expand* time; despite all the charges that *Jeanne d'Arc* imitates *Potemkin,* Dreyer has almost none of Eisenstein's fondness for prolonging an action by fragmenting it into many overlapping shots. Dreyer's temporal ellipsis, however, is consistent with his aim to concentrate on what is of fundamental importance: the essential is sufficient. Thus in *Jeanne d'Arc,* the action unfolds in what we might call an abstract duration, analogous to real time but more purified and intense, more dense with meaning.

The action also occupies a kind of abstract space. Contrary to many critics' claims, what the film generally lacks are not *long* shots (of which it has several) but rather *establishing* shots: images, distant or close, which place characters in space by reference to other characters, to settings, and to objects in the same frame. Some scenes have only a single establishing shot, at the very beginning; others (e.g., scenes two and five) have no establishing shots at all. As a result, Jeanne is almost never seen in a shot with other characters, but is instead isolated in her own frame. Moreover, in each scene, the area around the characters is gradually chopped away in a movement toward a spatial intensification and abstraction, a compression of the drama into a few symbolic images. At the beginning, a long shot will usually suggest the terrain of the scene, but immediately the action will be fragmented into medium shots and close-ups of single characters and objects. But since the purified decor doesn't offer common background elements to link the shots, and since the images are often set against each other in tense contrast (or "dialogue," in Jean Sémolué's term[6]), the images are often spatially discontinuous. Dreyer must consequently rely on the scene's narrative logic and rhythm and on the characters' glances to suggest spatial relations. At the same time, the repeated close-ups tend to minimize any sense of distance between the characters and to focus our attention on the nuances of the drama. The close-ups and cutting thus make the opposition of Jeanne and her judges not only concretely physical but also abstractly ideological. Every scene is stripped to its bare minimum, so that at the climax of each scene, a total meaning is telescoped into a few stark images—a face, a crown of reeds, a spike-studded wheel, a flock of birds, a stake. Space has been systematically condensed in order to concentrate on objects, gestures, and facial expression, thus giving the close-ups an even stronger valence as symbols than they have intrinsically.

The dialectic of concreteness and abstraction is maintained in yet another way. On one hand is Dreyer's use of point-of-view to link shots and to intensify and delimit our vision. Very often, a shot of a person's glance will be followed by a subjective shot; this process attempts to anchor the action concretely. In the first scene, for example, we witness a play of many viewpoints among Jeanne and the priests; in the second, the viewpoints are chiefly Jeanne's and Loyseleur's; in the torture chamber, our viewpoint is almost totally identified with Jeanne's. We need not here venture onto the theoretical problem of whether "subjective" shots approximate the way *we* really see; what is important is that such shots are conventional shorthand for what the *character* sees. Thus techniques of subjective camerawork and editing assert, on a new level, a tendency toward representational specificity.

Yet Dreyer's style again undermines this concreteness by abstraction. First, although certain shots are perhaps rough equivalents for a character's actual field of view, most of the film's "subjective" shots are not optically consistent. For example, in the first scene, when a judge looks across at Jeanne, we get a shot from his general direction but from a much closer vantage point than his. More striking are shots like the head-on subjective close-up of the shouting soldier, in which Dreyer uses a highly stylized rhythmic zoom-in and -out. Such strategies push even subjective techniques away from conventional representation and toward a pure shot-flow.

More important, Dreyer balances the specificity of subjectivity against a conceptual crosscutting. Not only does he cut between various actions in one locale (e.g., the opening scene) but he also crosscuts actions in various places: while Jeanne sits in her cell, her judges plot against her; as she recants, the English prepare the stake. As Griffith showed in *Intolerance,* such oppositions raise the action to a symbolic level, forcing us to make conceptual connections between the juxtaposed images. The crosscutting thus counterposes the concrete subjectivity to a more abstract omniscience.

In all, the form and style of *La Passion de Jeanne d'Arc* strive to impede cinema's representational functions, to transcend film's conventional concreteness and its ties to a temporal-spatial continuum by means of abstract images which are significant both in themselves and in the context of an elliptical, compressed narrative. In contrast, one thinks of Renoir's *La Règle du Jeu*, where nuances flash out from a welter of details streaming by like quicksilver; in *Jeanne d'Arc* all but a very few details are suppressed so that each nuance may be isolated, magnified, and probed. The opposition is not neat and is only one of degree: Renoir cannot escape the abstraction imposed by the frame, and Dreyer will not completely abandon the image's concrete, denotative capacities. Furthermore, since Dreyer treats stylistic norms in a unique way, his abstraction is to be defined not in relation to a Platonic ideal but rather in relation to conventions engendered by eighty years of filmmaking. Within a system of cinematic conventions, *Jeanne d'Arc*'s style respects the concrete physical integrity of people and objects and yet makes them images which are more pure, more intense, and more revelatory than reality.

This intense, stripped-down style is not just aesthetic parsimony, though; the dialectic of concreteness and abstraction is uncannily echoed in the dramatic conflict of earthly reality and spiritual vision. Externally, the clash is between the political maneuverings of the Church and the army and the visionary tenacity of Jeanne. Internally, Jeanne is divided: she must decide to accept either an earthly mission or a spiritual one. To the specific revelation of this conflict, in dramatic and visual terms, we shall now turn.

SCENE 1

> Note: So continuously fluid is the film that only with some arbitrariness can one break it into parts. I have chosen to demarcate changes of scene by shifts of locale because it does the least damage to the film's coherence. The reader should nevertheless

remember that the film contains no fades, dissolves, or other conventional transitions, so that the actual effect is of one long uninterrupted "scene."

The opening of *La Passion de Jeanne d'Arc* is a model of economy. The basic situation and mood are rendered swiftly and impressively; motifs which will appear later are given concise expression. Indeed, so dynamically are themes established in this opening scene that one would be tempted to call Dreyer's handling "musical" if the scene's construction did not depend so totally on composition, space, movement, decor, camera angle, and editing—on, that is, cinematic resources. The intricacy and compression of this opening demand a particularly detailed analysis.

A pair of gnarled hands turns the soiled pages of an old book: we are examining a record from the past. In the very next shot, that past comes vividly alive as we see priests settling in for Jeanne's trial. The paradoxical tension between the first two shots will recur throughout the film: we are seeing a historical event with a timeless immediacy.

The second shot defines the scope of the drama to come. As the camera tracks right, the priests in the foreground talk and take their seats; at the same time, in the middle distance a soldier sets a stool in the center of the room while soldiers in the far background lean on their spears and watch. The purely visual beauties of the shot—such as the way figures' behavior and camera movement are choreographed in an overall movement to the right, or the way the bright background etches the shadowy figures of the priests in sharp relief—are difficult to analyze verbally, but one can point out how the shot functions in the film's total form. First, Dreyer not only defines the locale of Jeanne's trial but also diagrams her essential situation: as the stool is midway between the priests and the soldiers, so she is caught between ecclesiastical and military authority, and both will try to trap her. Moreover, the fact that a soldier sets down the stool suggests that it is the English military who ultimately control the trial, a suggestion reinforced by the numerous soldiers in the background. Throughout this scene, alliances and oppositions among the characters will be revealed by means of spatial displacements within the three territories of judges, accused, and army plotted out in this first establishing shot.

At the same time Dreyer diagrams the political struggle behind the trial, he introduces—with an economy that becomes apparent only on several viewings—the judges who are to take part in the interrogations. In the long tracking shot we can glimpse the sepulchral Erard, who is to preach to Jeanne in the cemetery; Beaupère, with two tufts of hair like devil's horns; the imposing Pierre Cauchon, presiding judge; the fat, sinister Jean d'Estivet, who is to spit on Jeanne; the tall, cadaverous Nicholas Loyseleur (whose servility to Cauchon is suggested when the camera catches him bowing obediently); and the old white-haired priest who is to be one of Jeanne's allies. Significantly, the three ecclesiastics who will persecute Jeanne most brutally—Cauchon, Loyseleur, and d'Estivet—are all seen conferring together in this opening shot. Finally, the camera continues to track past the judges so that the last thing we see is the soldiers in the background, as if reminding us of the army's decisive power. In all, this incredible shot is analogous to the statement of a main theme in a musical composition: not only is it appealing in itself, but it also points our expectations toward future developments.

After surveying the entire terrain of the trial, Dreyer proceeds to analyze it; the conflict implicit in the planes of the tracking shot is now made explicit in the clashes *between* shots. Here is what follows the tracking shot I have been discussing:

3. (MS) Track up to Cauchon as he reads the charges.
4. (MS) The young monk Massieu, looking out to our left (toward Cauchon). He moves to our left as Jeanne enters the frame from the right.
5. (MS) Cauchon reading. (As 3.)

6. (MCU) Jeanne, head and shoulders, advancing to our left.
7. (MS) Cauchon reading. (As 3.)
8. (MCU) Jeanne advancing. (As 4.)
9. (MS) A priest's head rises into the frame; he looks down to our left.
10. (CU) Tracking shot: Jeanne's feet in chains, moving to the left.
11. (MS) Jeanne steps into the frame, looking straight out.
12. (LS) Her point-of-view: the tribunal, with the judges looking out at her.

These ten shots develop the drama in several ways. First, the clash of forces is rendered vividly by editing which opposes Jeanne and her judges; with these shots, crosscutting is established as a basic technique of continuity in the film. Notice, for instance, how the third and fourth shots generate visual conflict. The huge, grim, richly garbed figure of Cauchon is filmed from an imposing low angle; he and his colleagues' solid, round shapes darkly fill the frame. The next shot reveals the slender Massieu and the even smaller Jeanne, shot from a slightly high angle and framed by soldiers' spears; both are ascetically dressed and stand out against a patch of pure white. The graphic conflict of the shots establishes the tension of the drama: worldly authority versus spiritual strength. (In addition, the fourth shot foreshadows Massieu's eventual alignment with Jeanne at the end of the film.) At the same time, the opposition between shots is also one between stasis and movement, between shots of the unmoving judges (3, 5, 7) and of Jeanne advancing toward them (4, 6, 8). The shots of Jeanne also initiate Dreyer's characteristic use of movement in framing his close-ups: here and later in the film, the frame will be almost empty and the characters will move *into* it, as if the camera knew in advance where each action would end. Such deterministic framing traps the characters, creating an enclosed, claustrophobic effect. Moreover, we can see in this sequence the film's characteristic elliptical treatment of time and space, condensing a lengthy walk across a large room into a few brief close-ups. Finally, the clash of glances (Cauchon looking down to our right, Massieu and Jeanne looking up to our left) reinforces the thematic opposition and sets the key for the rest of the film, which will use the act of *looking* to define characters' spatial and dramatic relationships.

This act of looking is more explicitly present in shots 9–12. In the previous shots, the glances of the characters define their spatial positions and reveal their opposition, but now Dreyer uses techniques of subjective camerawork. As noted above, such shots are not optically valid (in real life, the priest would be too far away for Jeanne's feet to loom so large in his vision); but Dreyer draws on filmic convention to yield such "subjective" images in order to provide dramatic contexts for revealing close-ups. Thus the point-of-view shots prepare us for a style which will move freely from character to character, selecting this or that standpoint for maximum expressive impact. In all, in the first twelve shots, without including a word of dialogue, Dreyer introduces us to the dramatic world, thematic issues, and formal devices of his film.

The opening has sketched the basic situation. Jeanne is a prisoner, caught between the corrupt Church and the occupying army; but she is also a visionary who has pledged herself to God. Consequently, in the remainder of the first scene, two dramas are played in counterpoint: the political drama of a rigged trial and the spiritual drama of Jeanne's commitment to her vision. Both dramas are revealed by Dreyer's consummate dramatic sense, camerawork, compositions, editing, and point-of-view techniques.

From the start, the political and spiritual dramas begin to interweave. As Jeanne takes the oath, two priests watch her. One clasps his hands worriedly (later he will intervene on her behalf); the other priest picks dirt out of his ear, stares at his finger, and flicks the dirt away. But after these contrasting responses to the girl's spiritual sincerity, we are instantly confronted with the political meaning of the trial. Loyseleur looks across the room; the English general Warwick swaggers in. Wearing a helmet and chains draped across his uniform, he stands before a cluster of spears. (Throughout the film, Warwick's brutality will be associated with metal—chains, spears, helmets, grappling hooks, and maces.) Warwick exchanges glances with Loyseleur—the first concrete suggestion of the political alliance of army and Church which will develop further in the scene.

The personal drama comes to the fore again when Jeanne is questioned by Cauchon. Again, crosscutting, contrasting camera angles, and conflicting glances embody the characters' opposition. After questions about Jeanne's name and age, she is asked if she knows her Pater Noster. Instantly, Dreyer cuts to an extreme close-up of her: "Yes." "Who taught it to you?" Jeanne is silent. One priest leans forward; another barks out an oath. It is the first climax of Jeanne's spiritual drama and, appropriately, for the first time in the film, she turns her eyes toward heaven as she answers: "My mother. . . ." She breaks into tears and fiercely refuses to recite the Pater Noster. At one stroke, we see Jeanne as emotional, devout, and defiant—all traits she will manifest in the rest of the film.

But Jeanne has a political identity as well as a spiritual one. Does she claim that she has been sent by God to save France? Yes. The priests are variously amused and shocked. The judge La Fontaine asks if God hates the English and tightens his fist, as if squeezing Jeanne in a trap. She looks almost imperceptibly upward. "God hates no one"—she looks over her shoulder—"and I know that all the English will be chased out of France." Dreyer cuts to a close-up of the enraged Warwick and shortly thereafter pans from Warwick up to the cleric Nicholas Loyseleur standing behind him. The narrative economy is striking: Dreyer didn't need to show us Loyseleur plotting with Warwick or even crossing the room; Loyseleur's new position on the military side of the room and the surprise pan shot concisely reveal the Church's complicity in the English army's persecution. That persecution bursts out when Jeanne adds that all English will be driven out— "except those who die here." An English soldier jumps to his feet, shouting furiously at her, and Dreyer reinforces the shock of this by filming the soldier from Jeanne's point-of-view and zooming with dizzying speed in and out. Loyseleur intervenes and stands beetling over Jeanne like a cliff; her surprised stare suggests that she may be starting to regard him as a possible ally, which is precisely what he needs to achieve the trial's political end.

But immediately Dreyer returns to Jeanne's spiritual drama. Jeanne looks across the priests; while she is seen in static close-ups, tracking shots link them in opposition to her. Jeanne brilliantly parries their questions about St. Michael, leaving them discomfited. Does she want a dress? She replies that she will change into woman's clothes when her "mission" is done. The word reverberates ambiguously throughout the film. In one sense, Jeanne's mission is to drive the English out of France; that is the way the clergy, the English, and the French people conceive it. But Jeanne here sees her mission as not political but spiritual: God's answer will be "the salvation of my soul." Her mission may, then, be obedience to her God. The rest of the film will trace her difficult route toward the certainty of what her mission is.

But now the mammoth Jean d'Estivet is outraged by what he takes for blasphemy. In an astonishing sequence, he lumbers forward, bellows furiously at the girl, and spits on her cheek. So great is the tension that Dreyer builds by his quick cutting (over twenty brief shots), camera angles (low angles make d'Estivet look colossal), and close-ups (huge images of Jeanne's cheek and d'Estivet's lips) that the spittle which spatters onto her cheek has the dramatic force of an open-handed slap. Dreyer has carefully built to this moment: the growing impatience of the judges, the soldier's anger, and Jeanne's defiant and agile answers culminate in the first burst of violence in the film. Yet the violence, aside from its shock value, carries strong moral implications: Jeanne's stricken helplessness and wide, staring eyes, immobile before d'Estivet's gesture of contempt, create an unforgettable image of outraged human innocence.

Our sense of protest is immediately incarnated in the figure of de Houppeville, the monk who had pityingly watched Jeanne earlier in the scene. He rises and goes to her. "This isn't a trial. . . . It's a persecution!" Under the menacing eyes of d'Estivet and Cauchon, de Houppeville declares that he believes Jeanne is a saint and bows at her feet. (The ellipsis is vivid: we don't watch the monk bending over, only his head moving to touch the floor before Jeanne's chained feet.) The judges mock him for his humility, and a quick pan shot, linking the three conspirators Cauchon, Loyseleur, and d'Estivet, ominously suggests punishment in the offing for him.

At this point, Dreyer's method of channeling the flow of the drama by the characters' glances becomes dazzlingly intricate: he supplies us with a new fulcrum of point-of-view, the old white-haired priest whom we observed being helped to his seat in the beginning. Through this old priest's eyes we view the process by which Church and army combine to silence de Houppeville. The old priest watches a revealing drama: Warwick gives an order to his aide, who crosses the room to Loyseleur, speaks briefly to him, and returns to Warwick. The old priest's attention shifts to another part of the room. A sudden close-up of moving spears and helmets suggests the soldiers are filing out the door. With the consent of the Church, de Houppeville has been arrested by Warwick's men. Henry James would have admired Dreyer's powerful obliqueness: instead of dialogue revealing Warwick's and Loyseleur's conspiracy, we get the action filtered through the consciousness of a witness. Dreyer's use of point-of-view, aided by the ominous detail of the soldiers' spears, makes the scene's drama more concentrated, subtle, and intense.

The army's intervention makes explicit what was hinted in the film's opening: Warwick wields the ultimate power in this court. This shocks some judges into dissent. As the soldiers' spears troop out, cut in close-ups show priests' faces rising abruptly into the frame. (Again Dreyer builds a sense of opposition by the graphic clash of the left-to-right movement of the spears and the upward movements of the faces.) The old priest protests, but Cauchon shouts him down and orders the other dissenting judges to reseat themselves.

As if to conceal this blatant political maneuvering, Cauchon pursues questions about spiritual matters. Has God made Jeanne any promises? Although Jeanne says yes, her eyes turn upward and widen mysteriously. "You are not real judges. Take me to the Pope in Rome." Cauchon jovially takes a vote of the judges' opinion of their authority. The camera tracks down the judges' raised hands to end on one young priest, Martin Ladvenu, who is bullied by Cauchon's frown into raising his hand too. Cauchon looks back at Jeanne and asks her if God promised her that she would be saved. The following close-up of her is an intense, extreme one making the frame itself a kind of imprisonment of Jeanne's face— the aesthetic equivalent for the suffocating pressure of the question. Jeanne lifts her head and, staring intently upward, agrees that God will save her. But her spirits immediately sink as she adds: "I know neither the day nor the hour." Cauchon's patience has run out: a tracking shot rushes away from him as he shouts that the session is closed. Parallel to the tracking shot at the very beginning, the camera now moves left down the judges as they rise to leave the court. Cauchon and his collaborators fume as Jeanne is led out; as in her first shot, she is flanked by spears (a reminder that her adversaries are prepared to use violence if necessary). Still more tracking shots follow Loyseleur and Warwick as they walk past the conferring judges and discuss Jeanne's fate. "She slips out of our grasp. Must we trick her?"

Taken as a whole, this opening scene has an extraordinary richness. Dreyer has delineated the essential forces of the drama. On one side is Jeanne, with her mystical fervor and rebellious will; her allies are Massieu, the arrested de Houppeville, the protesting old priest, and the young Ladvenu. On the other side are the Church and the English army, determined to see that Jeanne does not escape. Dreyer has distinctly characterized each major figure of authority; the explosive Cauchon, the gross d'Estivet, the quietly sinister Loyseleur, and the vengeful but distant Warwick represent a range of responses to Jeanne. In this first scene, too, we have seen the violence and hatred of which the Church and the army are capable. Moreover, Dreyer has established crosscutting, close-ups, elliptical editing, stylized decor, subjective camerawork, and shifting point-of-view as the film's principal stylistic strategies for revealing conflict, tightening suspense, concentrating and abstracting time and space, and suggesting spirituality. Perhaps most important, the initial tension between worldly authority and spiritual vision states the crucial dilemma facing Jeanne. Is her mission political or spiritual? Is she to save France or her soul? It is her movement toward resolving the dilemma that is the central theme of the ensuing film.

SCENE 2

In this scene, the principle of crosscutting shifts to a new level. Whereas earlier Dreyer had used it to trace out the arteries of an action occurring in a single location, now he crosscuts scenes occurring simultaneously in two places. As before, the principle of contrast rules. While Jeanne is in her cell, the judges conspire to trick her with a forged letter. Dreyer reveals the authorities' complicity by shots which pan from Loyseleur dictating to the scribe's pen, from the scribe to Cauchon, and—most telling of all—across the judges to the shadow of Warwick pacing in the distance: it is he who controls. In contrast to this corruption is Jeanne's purity; while the authorities forge a letter concerning her political mission, she takes spiritual comfort from the shadow of the cross made by the bars of her cell window and begins to plait a crown of straw. The objects are important. The crown of straw implies that Jeanne expects martyrdom; at the climax of the film, she will see this crown as a sign of her true mission. In addition, besides suggesting Jeanne's likeness to Christ, the cross-shadow shows her transforming her imprisonment into a symbol of grace. Her ability to make such a transformation represents the first step toward her resolution of the tension between earthly and spiritual commitments.

The contrast of corruption and purity is reinforced by the abrupt entry of the guards, who mock Jeanne and try to seize her ring. The soldier's assault of Jeanne foreshadows both the judges' verbal assault and the subsequent torture. (One shot—the close-up of the soldier's hand wrenching Jeanne's arm around—renders an excruciatingly painful moment as also an abstract image of brutality.) Loyseleur intervenes (seen from Jeanne's viewpoint), dismisses the guards, and returns Jeanne's ring to her. His intervention is well-timed, for it helps convince Jeanne that he is her friend. But Dreyer obliterates any doubts about Loyseleur's actual nature by showing his shadow blocking out the shadow of the cross. Although Jeanne is momentarily persuaded of his sincerity when he claims to have "great pity" for her, again Dreyer undercuts Loyseleur's imposture by a swooping tracking shot that reveals Cauchon at a peephole, spying on the scene. Finally, Loyseleur wins over Jeanne completely by reading her the letter purportedly from King Charles. When Jeanne hears that Charles plans to march on Rouen with a large army, she smiles peacefully. Thus she is not disturbed when the judges bustle into her cell; her wildly staring eyes suggest that she sees God's promise on the verge of fulfillment; her deliverance—an earthly one, a rescue by Charles —seems near at hand.

In the ensuing interrogation, the opposition between Jeanne and the judges which was established in the first scene is restated in more intense terms. Here, Jeanne and the authorities are never seen in the same shot; Dreyer constructs the space of the drama by cutting among the characters' glances. Jeanne is the center of attention: when she looks to our right, her attention is focused on the questioner; when she looks to our left, the next shot is of Loyseleur, who is supposedly her ally; and at the climax of the scene, when Loyseleur abandons her, Jeanne's eyes turn toward heaven. Thus Dreyer has no need for establishing shots; he need only suggest the spatial organization in order to concentrate on the nuances of expression that create the scene's primary movement. By such cutting and close-ups and with the aid of the purified backgrounds, the drama is stripped to its bare essentials—the characters and their expressions.

The scene traces the partial success and ultimate frustration of the judges' efforts to trick Jeanne. At first her trust of Loyseleur leads her into more and more damning admissions. After reciting the Pater Noster, she is asked if God promised her she would be released. Her eyes widen and she smiles joyously as she answers yes. "By a great victory?" asks another priest. Again she affirms it; she assumes that the letter from Charles has confirmed God's promise of this victory. But she becomes uneasy at the increasing gravity of the questions. "Did God promise you that you would go to heaven?" Trembling, she looks to Loyseleur; he nods for her to answer yes; she confidently does so. "Then you're sure of being saved?" Confused, she turns again to Loyseleur, who nods; again she answers yes. But the young Brother Massieu (whose sympathy for Jeanne was suggested in the first scene) comes forward to warn her: "Take care; it's a very serious answer." The interrogator Beaupère and Cauchon shout for Massieu to be silent, and he worriedly obeys.

With the tension at this pitch, the questions become still more aggressive. Beaupère turns grimly to Jeanne. "Since you believe one can be saved without help, perhaps you wish to give up the Sacrament." Jeanne swallows, moistens her lips, and turns her eyes beseechingly to Loyseleur. But he merely stares back at her. Jeanne's eyes fill with tears. Two priests lean anxiously forward as Beaupère puts the fatal question:

"Are you in a state of grace?"

Trembling, Jeanne wets her lips and looks quickly left to Loyseleur. He turns away from her, staring straight out. Her eyes beg him for help, but he will not meet her gaze. She is abandoned.

"Well?" snaps Beaupère. "Answer! Are you in a state of grace?"

Jeanne's eyes turn slowly toward heaven. Two priests recoil in shock. Before our eyes, Jeanne's face beatifies. Her head tilted back, her eyes staring intently, she answers tranquilly: "If I am, may God keep me there. If I am not, may God put me there." In the course of the questioning, we have seen Jeanne move away from a confidence in Loyseleur and King Charles toward fear, doubt, and despair, and finally to a serene trust in God. The shift of her glance from the world of men to the realm of the spirit expresses the ability of her faith to transcend earthly bonds.

As if to make this vision concrete, Jeanne begs to hear the Mass. But Cauchon refuses—unless she will give up wearing men's clothes. The opposition of the two characters is reinforced by the terrific strain between shots of Jeanne's body stooped over sidewise and Cauchon's huge, looming figure. Jeanne looks again to the left for advice, and now in place of the deceiving Loyseleur stands Massieu, shortly joined by the young priest Ladvenu. They advise her to do as Cauchon says. But Jeanne shakes her head. Cauchon shouts at her; Massieu pleads with her; she looks frantically from one to the other; the cutting rate increases sharply, with almost twenty shots assaulting the viewer in just a few moments. Finally Cauchon denounces her as not "the daughter of God" but "the tool of Satan," and a single tear trickles down her cheek. Jeanne, sobbing, watches the judges file out of her cell.

Immediately, like a composer repeating a theme in a new key,

Dreyer supplies an echo of the interrogation we have just witnessed. As the judges leave, Jeanne's guards enter and begin to mock her. One tickles her cheek with a straw, plays with her straw crown, and claps it on her head; another supplies an arrow as a scepter. The episode's cutting is confusing; again, there is no establishing shot revealing the entire cell, but whereas during the previous interrogation Dreyer kept all spatial coordinates absolutely consistent, this mockery episode muddles viewpoints and directions of glances and movements. For the only time in the film, Dreyer neglects to make his characters' position in the shot unambiguously define their spatial locations, so that at times we are not certain about where the guards stand in relation to Jeanne.

But if the cutting sometimes confuses, the scene's narrative significance is clear. Jeanne's likeness to Jesus, earlier suggested by the cross images and the crown, is here made explicit by the guards' mockery, with the straw as an analog for the centurion's spear. Moreover, the previous interrogation is grotesquely parodied by the brutish guards. The behavior of the most mocking guard reiterates, with sarcasm, Cauchon's behavior: the guard's cupping his hands around his eye to study Jeanne recalls Cauchon's peephole scrutiny, and Cauchon's denunciation of her is repeated in the guard's sneer, "She looks like a real daughter of God!" Finally, one guard's casual use of his sword to twirl and toss her crown into the air suggests—as the judges' determination to trap and torture her suggested—that Jeanne will suffer still more at the hands of authority. Just as the porter's speech in *Macbeth* recapitulates by parody the motifs in Macbeth's earlier speeches, so here the guards' actions become a coarser version of the judges' persecution. And, as in the interrogation, it is Massieu who comes to Jeanne's aid, dismissing the guards and going to comfort her. The scene ends brilliantly: when Dreyer finally includes someone in the same shot as Jeanne, it is, appropriately, Massieu, who sits down beside her, carefully removes her crown and scepter, and wipes her tears on his sleeve.

As a whole, this second scene has moved the drama onto several new levels. The crosscutting has become more complex, the use of glance more intricate. Two brief scenes of the guards' torment of Jeanne have framed the judges' interrogation; all three episodes have forcefully shown the deceptiveness, ruthlessness, and violence of the authorities. Jeanne has been identified with Christ, in contrast to the tyrannical judges and the brutish guards. Massieu has emerged as her most steadfast ally, but even he is powerless. The cross image and the crown have suggested that perhaps Jeanne's very imprisonment is a potential route to her salvation. Most important, Jeanne has revealed her ability to transcend this world and to trust in another world. That trust is put to a more severe test in the next scene.

SCENE 3

The opening of the third scene echoes that of the first scene in several respects. First, we are given a multiplaned long shot to establish the spatial coordinates: judges enter the torture chamber and seat themselves in the foreground, and soon a door in the distance opens to admit Massieu and Jeanne. (The Christ motif is recalled in the two crossed boards leaning against the rear wall, on the same plane as Jeanne.) Again, as in the beginning, subjectivity is introduced: Dreyer cuts to a shot which, by tracking left and panning right, reveals the torturer, his machines, and his fire as seen from Jeanne's point-of-view. And as a soldier in the opening had set a stool in the center of the court, so now a cleric brings out a stool for Jeanne. But far from being mere repetition, these echoes of the first scene accumulate intensity and embody the growing seriousness of Jeanne's plight. First, the open, apparently impartial courtroom of the first scene is here replaced by the constricted, foreboding torture chamber—a sinister shift which Dreyer emphasizes in the way the dark shapes of the judges in the foreground press in on the distant, diminutive figure of Jeanne. Similarly, the delicate and complex network of observers' points-of-view in the first scene is here reduced to an identification solely with Jeanne. And although in the first scene the soldier had dragged the stool across matter-of-factly, as observed from a high long shot, the cleric in this scene is viewed from a frightening low angle as he brandishes the stool over his head like a club. By cinematic means, Dreyer has both recapitulated and intensified the first scene's air of inquisition; the shots prepare us for the most threatening assault on Jeanne yet.

The note of exhortation in the previous scene is struck in this interrogation too, and builds to a tense climax. The monk who brings the stool has the smiling face of one who submits to authority ("Don't you think these learned men are wiser than you?"), while another questioner invokes the superiority of ecclesiastical wisdom ("Your revelations do not come from God . . ."). At first Jeanne is shocked by the suggestion that she has been deceived by a demon, but soon, without a word, she simply smiles: she knows she knelt to St. Michael, not Satan. Her quiet confidence infuriates the priests; as in the previous scene, the characters' positions are defined by glance, gesture, cutting and Jeanne's point-of-view; and the close-ups and tracking shots of the shouting priests, whose faces punch fiercely into the frame, contrast almost viscerally with the calm, static close-ups of Jeanne's face. She is given the recantation and a pen. As Massieu watches, Jeanne stares up at the lunging, bellowing faces of the judges and shakes her head. She will not admit that her visions are unholy. Her interrogator warns her: "Your judges are offering you a helping hand." He stands up and, from a steep low angle representing Jeanne's viewpoint, he adds: "If you refuse it, they will abandon you to the English executioner and you will be left alone." Jeanne smiles. "Alone!" repeats the judge. "Yes, alone!" she answers. "Alone with God!"

It is a good index of Dreyer's dramatic skill that he immediately tests this affirmation of Jeanne's belief in her vision. The questioner looks to the left, and in a frightening yet virtually abstract image, the silhouette of a heavy iron chain moves slowly up the frame to reveal at its end a huge grappling hook. Thus begins one of the most dazzling sequences in the entire film: sixty-nine separate shots whose rhythmic editing is virtuosic. But in contrast to the idle quick-cutting-for-its-own-sake of much contemporary movie-making, Dreyer's sequence is profoundly expressive: its point-of-view shots and dynamically edited close-ups constitute the most intense presentation so far of Jeanne's experience. The sequence may be divided into three phases:

1. Terrified, Jeanne glances across the torture apparatus: squirting water, whirling spiked rollers, sliding sawteeth, and a huge spiked wheel cranked by the torturer. Various point-of-view shots of these machines are linked by Jeanne's shifting glance, which finally fastens on the spinning torture wheel. Intensely close shots of the spikes on the wheel whizzing past are followed by flashes of the torturer's figure glimpsed through the wheel's spokes. This entire series of shots concretely expresses the threat at the judges' disposal.

2. The judges demand that Jeanne recant; while the wheel whirls in the background, one priest grabs her wrist and thrusts the recantation at her. When Jeanne looks back at the horrible wheel, the pace of the cutting and the speed of the wheel increase. Images of the bellowing Cauchon are juxtaposed to those of the whizzing spikes. Jeanne turns to the judges and cries: "Even if you separate my soul from my body, I will revoke nothing. And if I say anything later, I shall say that I was forced to speak."

3. The pace accelerates climactically. The cutting connects close-ups of Jeanne's staring face, close-ups of the spikes, flashes of the torturer's figure, and close-ups of Jeanne's hand holding the pen. The juxtaposition of Jeanne's face (seen head-on) with the whizzing spikes (also seen head-on) creates a slashing sensation, as if she were about to be ripped open. Dreyer orchestrates the

flashing images by means of repetitions and collisions of shape, movement, and speed: e.g., from the static shot of the pen held at a slanting angle, Dreyer cuts to a shot of the spiked wheel moving at a similar angle, and then cuts back to the pen as it droops to a different angle in Jeanne's hand. The tempo builds to a climax— a fusillade of close-ups, each only a second or two long—and Jeanne faints, falling at Cauchon's feet. As he looks down disgustedly, the torturer and a monk bend over Jeanne and prepare to take her back to her cell.

This swiftly-paced sequence (the average shot is about two seconds long) systematically strips to the essentials the conflict which emerged during the interrogation. In the first part of the scene, the camera explored all the faces of Jeanne's judges, but by the end, Cauchon's face suffices to symbolize the entire force of the judges' wrath. Similarly, Dreyer had earlier surveyed the menacing variety of torture devices; but by the end, he needs only the spiked wheel to symbolize the clergy's appeal to violence. The sequence works on two levels: Cauchon remains first of all a shouting man and the wheel remains a wheel, but the logic of the narrative and Dreyer's progressive intensification raises Cauchon and the wheel to the status of signs, representing the alternatives which the judges offer Jeanne. Thus the violence prefigured in the first scene and barely warded off in the second comes perilously close to bursting out in this scene. Yet opposed to this threat of physical suffering is Jeanne's unyielding commitment to her spiritual vision, her willingness to split her soul from her body if that is necessary to remain faithful to her God. We are tensely prepared for the judges to take even harsher measures to break her resistance.

SCENE 4

Jeanne has fainted and is taken back to her cell, where Massieu supervises the soldiers' setting up of her bed. (Here the authorities' ignoring Jeanne's spiritual mission is concisely expressed in the casual flip with which one soldier tosses Jeanne's crown to the floor.) Jeanne awakes to see Warwick at her bedside, and her first close view of the man who controls her trial is subjective, emphasizing his power over her. But the confrontation comes to nothing. Jeanne closes her eyes wearily while Warwick warns the doctor: "She must not die a natural death. The King of England has paid dearly for her."

In Scene 2, Dreyer had repeatedly cut from the judges forging the letter to Jeanne's prayers. It is a measure of the degree which Jeanne's strength has waned that now Dreyer crosscuts shots of Cauchon, Loyseleur, and Warwick plotting on the staircase with shots of the doctor's bleeding of Jeanne. The latter image, while immediately painful (most audiences wince audibly at this point) is raised to a conceptual level by being juxtaposed with the authorities' plans to drain Jeanne's resistance by torture if necessary. Indeed, Dreyer cements the connection by repeating movement from shot to shot: as Loyseleur and Warwick come into the frame from the left, so does the doctor's knife in the next shot, and Loyseleur's later movement out of the frame is repeated in the spurting arc of Jeanne's blood. The conventional connotation of blood as vitality reinforces our impression of the judges gradually gaining power over Jeanne's life.

To extend this power, Cauchon comes in to interrogate Jeanne again. The conflict between Jeanne and Cauchon articulated in the vibrant montage sequence in the previous scene shifts to a more intimate tension here—reinforced, as we would expect, by glance and subjective point-of-view. As Jeanne sleeps, Cauchon studies her thoughtfully. When she awakes, Cauchon smiles at her and the other judges file into the cell. As in other scenes, a single establishing shot presents the dramatic space in its entirety before the ensuing drama is played in close-ups. Jeanne is afraid that she will die and begs that her body be put in holy ground. Cauchon assures her that the Church welcomes back its lost sheep, but Dreyer immediately cancels any possibility of Cauchon's being merciful: Jeanne's hand reaches desperately into the frame, trying to clasp Cauchon's hand, but he disgustedly draws away. In this one gesture, Dreyer reveals a man so emotionally dead that his reflexes won't permit him to even mimic compassion.

The new threat we have been tensely awaiting comes when, from Jeanne's point-of-view, we see Massieu and the scribe setting up a communion altar. A priest enters. Jeanne is joyful; she will at least die a good Christian. As in the second scene, the drama consists of the interplay of glances and gestures caught in close-up: Jeanne watches the priest and imitates him in making the sign of the cross; when he turns around and holds up the wafer, her head strains desperately toward it. But at exactly the same moment, the scribe matter-of-factly thrusts the recantation toward her hand. Now, after various kinds of torture have failed, the Church ruthlessly uses Christ's body as a new way to torment Jeanne. "Do you know," asks Cauchon sternly, "that this is the body of your Lord? Can't you see that you are offending God?" The camera follows Jeanne's glance as it sweeps along the circle of judges; she looks toward the wafer; then she looks at the recantation. Dreyer's use of close-ups and economical visual symbols, linked by point-of-view, perfectly realizes Jeanne's dilemma: a close-up of the recantation, followed by a huge close-up of Jeanne's anguished face turning to the right and then by an extreme close-up of the wafer—these three shots embody the essence of the scene. Jeanne must sign the recantation or deny the Church.

She denies the Church. After she pushes the recantation away, the priest turns around, the wafer vanishes, and the judges start to leave. Jeanne is frantic. "I love God! I love him with all my heart." The judges fiercely shout her down, calling her "the devil's instrument." For a moment she submits to their wrath, but she again summons up enough strength to defy them. "It's you," she sobs, "who have been sent by the devil to make me suffer." Again, Dreyer reinforces the dramatic conflict by graphic impact: close-ups of Jeanne looking up to the right collide with close-ups of the judges looking down to the left. Cauchon shouts: "There's nothing more to do. . . . Have the English call their executioner." The judges leave Jeanne weeping and rubbing her face desperately. We have not before seen her so shattered.

Again the drama has moved to a new level. In refusing to recant, even under the threat of losing communion, Jeanne rejects the religious authority of her accusers. In earlier scenes, Jeanne defiantly asserted her spirtual identity, but now she holds its power above that of the Church. Theological disputation is now pointless. The judges must expose what has been implicit throughout: the threat of death at the hands of the English army. And now that Jeanne has passed beyond the Church's domain, she must face the deepest dilemma of all: what is the nature of her mission?

SCENE 5

At this point we should recall that the film's action runs on two levels. At the political level, the struggle is between Jeanne's obstinate refusal to recant and the political maneuvering of the judges and Warwick. For the most part, this is an external drama, emphasized in the graphic clash of Jeanne and her judges (close-ups, reverse shots, crosscutting). But a spiritual drama runs parallel to this political drama. Besides Jeanne's resistance to ever more fierce external assaults, we have glimpsed a harrowing inner struggle. In the first scene, Jeanne announced that her mission was spiritual ("the salvation of my soul"), but she also revealed her uncertainty at the close of the scene, when, though asserting that she will be saved, she added morosely: "I know neither the day nor the hour." The second scene revealed her confusion even more clearly: the message that Charles' army was advancing seemed to promise her that she would indeed be freed by the "great victory" God had promised; the deliverance God had promised would be the saving of her life. At the same time, her defiance of torture proved that she is prepared to be "alone with God." Yet, as Scene 5 suggested, she feels profoundly anguished about disobeying the Church. And in physical terms, her alternating moods of confidence and despair reveal the intensity of the struggle within her. In short, although Jeanne clings to her mission, she has not yet discovered exactly what that mission is. In the fifth scene of the film, before a crowd in Rouen cemetery, Jeanne is forced to define her mission.

The opening of the cemetery scene summarizes and intensifies several motifs already established in the film. There is the threat of violence, suggested by the first long-shot of the shadows of the soldiers with their maces, dominating the crowd. The army's control of the entire town is revealed in the positioning of guards to restrain the people. The torture wheels on poles behind the crowd recall the spiked machine in the torture chamber. As Cauchon and the other judges stride sternly through the crowd to the tribunal, we see their authority reasserted before the entire populace. When Jeanne is carried out on a stretcher, Massieu walks at her side, reminding us of his entrance in the first scene. Similarly, the alliance of Loyseleur and Warwick is restated when the two come out into the courtyard together. The soldier's attack on Jeanne in the first scene is now magnified in the powerful shot from behind Jeanne's back, revealing her facing a tower full of soldiers. And the various tormentors that have harried Jeanne throughout the film are recalled in the single dispassionate figure of the old gravedigger. As befits such a crucial scene, Dreyer here reintroduces the key dramatic elements and starts building them to a new pitch.

The wizened Erard mounts the podium and launches a new attempt to persuade Jeanne to reçant. While the crowd and

Jeanne's allies (Massieu, Ladvenu, and the old priest who had protested in the first scene) look on, Erard tells Jeanne that her king is a heretic. Jeanne is trembling but is controlled enough to smile and reply: "My King is a better Christian than you!" Significantly, Jeanne's alliance here is to an earthly king, to whom her earthly mission was devoted. But while Erard continues to harangue her about pride, Jeanne abruptly realizes the importance of her choice. As we would expect in this most visual of dramas, her dilemma is expressed by glances which link objects:

46. (CU) Jeanne looks down.
47. (CU) Dirt is tossed up from a grave.
48. (CU) Jeanne, looking.
49. (CU) A skull is tossed up and lands on the dirt at the edge of the grave.
50. (CU) Jeanne's eyes widen.
51. (CU) Another shovelful of dirt tumbles over the skull.
52. (CU) Jeanne looks to our lower left.
53. (MS) Loyseleur watches.
54. (CU) Jeanne's glance moves slowly to our right.
55. (MS) Track left down flowers growing by wall.
56. (MS) Jeanne shifts her eyes to our right.
57. (ECU) Skull: eye socket.
58. (MS) Jeanne looks, her eyes widening.
59. (ECU) Skull: a worm crawls in the eye socket.

By the cutting, the movement of Jeanne's eyes, and the flower–skull opposition, Dreyer has delineated the necessity of Jeanne's choosing between survival and execution, and the barely-moving worm in the eye socket brings her face to face with the concrete horror of death.

Jeanne hesitates. The clerk hands her the recantation. Erard shakes his fist and cries: "The executioner is waiting!" As Jeanne looks, the camera tracks past a bored-looking man sitting on a cart, then swoops up through smoke to a heavy grappling hook, swinging ominously. (Cf. the torture sequence.) Jeanne has already confronted death's finality; now she is reminded of its agony. At this moment, Loyseleur intervenes with a plea that has not been heard before: "You have no right to die. . . . You must still fight for your country!" Jeanne, wavering, looks dazedly toward Warwick; behind him, soldiers stand in a tower, spears at the ready. And now her allies—Massieu, Ladvenu, the old priest—shout: "Jeanne, sign!" It is decisive. Jeanne chooses to save her life. She shakily signs the recantation.

But she is not to be freed. Cauchon rises to read Jeanne's sentence. The ironies pile up: "Since you recognize your crime, you are no longer a criminal. . . . But since you sinned rashly, we condemn you"—Jeanne's face quivers—"to life imprisonment, with the bread of affliction and the water of sorrow." Jeanne smiles, trembling. Loyseleur congratulates her: "You have saved your life and your soul!" As Jeanne leaves, the judges smile among themselves. But Warwick is not satisfied: when Loyseleur brings him the recantation, Warwick furiously slaps it away. "This sorceress has fooled you . . . but I know how to force her to betray herself." Even more ominous is the way the crowd's jubilation is restrained by the soldiers: crossed spears fence the people in, and one man who struggles is grabbed by two soldiers and hurled into a pool of water. It is a foreboding of what is to come in the final scene.

This scene is, then, critically important because Jeanne chooses life over death. The preciousness of life (the flowers), the grim finality of death (the skull), the pain of torture, the possibility that she may lead an army again, and the urgings of her sympathizers—all convince Jeanne that her mission is an earthly one, to serve her king and country by surviving at all costs. In the next scene, the climax of Jeanne's spiritual drama, she will discover that this conception of her mission is utterly false.

SCENE 6

A snip of hair—the most famous bit of hair in all cinema—
falls to the floor. An impassive guard shears Jeanne's head as a
sign of penitence. The following close-up of Jeanne's tearful face
marks the logical culmination of the film's thematic and stylistic
progress: the judges, who have tried to strip Jeanne of her man's
clothes and of her courage, now order her head shaved; at the
same time, there is now one less element in Dreyer's mise-en-
scène, and Jeanne's face stands out even more nakedly than
before. Visually, the image typifies the film's incredible poise between the abstract (Jeanne's shaved head as an emblem of suffering) and the concrete (the almost physical force of her face).
This brief scene usually remains in viewers' memories long after
the film is over, perhaps because a series of more and more
serious attempts at torture has prepared us to see in a simple
snip of hair a terrifying image of authority's attempt to alter one's
very self. Even physical violence seems less horrifying than this
spiritual violence, this ultimate assault on the individual's identity.

But, consistently with the rest of the film, Dreyer crosscuts
the scene of Jeanne's humiliation with the celebration of the
townspeople at a fair. The contrast is in mood (the crowd's
festivity–Jeanne's agony) and in theme: the contortionists and
sword-swallowers enact make-believe pain, while Jeanne's suffering is intensely real. The theme of violence is taken further
when the camera glides over a man balancing a wheel on his
head; we are reminded of the torture wheels in the back of
several shots. It is possible to object that this crosscutting dis-
tracts us from Jeanne's scene, but as usual, Dreyer wants to
present the specific elements as vividly as possible and at the
same time to generate a more abstract connection. By these cuts,
Jeanne's fate is both differentiated from and linked to the
crowd's; the people's amusements parody her torture but also
foreshadow the violence that will eventually engulf everyone.

When the barber is done, he blows his scissors clean and sweeps up while the numb Jeanne sits beneath her cross-shaped window. She watches as her hair is swept up. The broom casually slides her discarded crown of straw across the floor and flips it into the dustpan with the bits of hair. It is a tremendously important moment: in accepting imprisonment, she has been shorn of grace as certainly as of her hair. Contrary to what Loyseleur had said, she cannot save both her life and her soul. This simple close-up of the crown, the hair, and the broom beautifully poses the tension between earthly and spiritual demands that has haunted Jeanne. At this moment, Jeanne changes her mind; she chooses the eternal. "Get the judges!"

As English soldiers prepare the stake, the judges assemble in Jeanne's cell. Trembling, she confesses: "I renounced God to save my life!" Jeanne now sees that fear had blinded her to her real mission. In the first interrogation, she had claimed that she was born to save France, and it was Loyseleur's reminding her of this that had helped determine her signing of the recantation. But in choosing to live at her captors' mercy, she implicitly denied her true self—the Jeanne that grasped a vision of order beyond this world of fear and imprisonment. Now the judges' cunning gives way to astonishment. Cauchon is almost compassionate: "So you believe you are a messenger from God?" Jeanne nods tearfully and closes her eyes. A scribe records her reply. "Fatal answer!" breathes Massieu. Even d'Estivet, who had spit and raged at her in the first scene, cannot withhold tears. Cauchon closes his eyes and moves away sorrowfully. Dreyer will not withhold humanity even from these corrupt men: they are at least capable of recognizing the grace they lack. At the same time, brusquely cut-in shots of the soldiers preparing the execution remind us that Jeanne's fate is now determined.

Jeanne is left alone with the young Massieu and Ladvenu. "We've come to prepare you for death." When Massieu tells her she is sentenced to death at the stake, her cheek twitches and she looks down. Ladvenu leaves to get the communion service. Massieu, who has tried several times to save Jeanne, still does not understand her. His questioning defines Jeanne's recognition of her true mission:

111. (CU) Massieu leans forward.
112. "Tell me, how can you still believe you've been sent by God?"
113. (CU) Massieu.
114. (ECU) Jeanne, staring, speaks.
115. "God knows where he is leading us. We see the road only at the end of our trip."
116. (ECU) Jeanne.
117. (CU) Massieu, leaning forward, nods.
118. (ECU) Jeanne smiles.
119. "Yes, I am his child."
120. (ECU) Jeanne.
121. (CU) Massieu, chest heaving.
122. (ECU) Jeanne smiling.
123. (CU) Massieu asks, "And the great victory?"
124. (MS) Jeanne lifts her eyes and head. "It will be my martyrdom."
125. (CU) Massieu. "And your deliverance?"
126. (MS) Jeanne looks up. "Death!"

These alternating shots of the hard-breathing Massieu and the tearful but radiant Jeanne climax the drama of question-and-answer that has been central to the film, but now the interrogator has no political motives: Massieu is the first to inquire seriously into Jeanne's spiritual condition. What emerges in this final interrogation is that only when faced with death ("the end of our trip") does Jeanne grasp the real meaning of her life. Seeing her crown and hair swept out made her realize that choosing to live was a repudiation of her vision. She now understands that her mission is not earthly but spiritual. Her victory will not be a military one, and her deliverance will not be by King Charles' hand; her victory is her self-sacrifice for her vision, and her deliverance will issue from that. In recognizing her martyrdom she recognizes her true self; in accepting death, she (like Christ) asserts the ultimate validity of her existence. Just as the shadow of her cell bars became the sign of the cross, so now her execution will become her victory. The personal drama overrides the political one: only by dying can Jeanne fulfill her life.

Again, Dreyer imbeds Jeanne's situation in a wider context by crosscutting her communion with the crowd's learning of her new recantation. The still, quiet resignation of the close-ups of Jeanne praying is in tense contrast to the hectic long shots of the people swarming into Rouen Castle. Dreyer's upside-down shots of the crowd may seem jarring, but at this point the film needs a leap into a new dimension, a quantum jump of visual energy that will impel us toward the ferocity of the ending. Already, in these uneasy overhead shots, the clash of crowd and soldiers is foreshadowed.

Yet the restless scope of these shots doesn't blur Dreyer's intensely individual focus. Fittingly, it is Jeanne's most faithful ally, Massieu, who gives her communion. As she prays, Loyseleur pauses outside her cell. In previous establishing shots, we have seen Jeanne in the distance, locked in by the figures of the menacing clergy in the foreground. Now Jeanne is seen praying in long shot, but this time she is framed by a ring of choirboys and arches; Loyseleur and some soldiers stand in the darker foreground, as if shut out from the luminous holiness radiating from Jeanne. And when Loyseleur turns away trembling from Jeanne's acceptance of communion, we are reminded of his betrayal of her in this very cell; Dreyer's habitual shot/reverse-shot cutting now measures the gulf between Jeanne's sanctity and Loyseleur's guilt.

Dreyer has, then, forcefully presented Jeanne's zealous choice of death and linked it to the curious crowd and the brutal army. In deciding to die for her vision, Jeanne has chosen a private destiny, but, as the final scene shall show, it has the most explosive public repercussions.

SCENE 7

In this final scene, the threads of the film's thematic and formal development are tightly entwined. Again, the musical metaphor is appropriate: the theme of Jeanne's spiritual drama is given full statement; a bridge passage carries us to the political consequences of her martyrdom; and a coda restates the main theme. The analogy should not be pushed too far, but the fluidity of Dreyer's development of visual and dramatic motifs and his exact control of tempo and rhythm remind us that a film can find a temporal form unlike that of the drama or the novel.

At first, the focus is on Jeanne, with occasional reminders of the crowd and the soldiers. Crosscutting juxtaposes close-ups of Jeanne's feet walking through the castle with swift tracking shots of the soldiers fastening chains to contain the crowd. (We recall that chains bound Jeanne's feet and dangled from Warwick's uniform in the first scene.) Jeanne emerges from the castle, flanked by a fence of spears. The people's support of Jeanne is emphasized when an old woman comes forward to give her a drink. Warwick takes a seat above his soldiers, who are depersonalized as a cluster of helmets behind him. As Jeanne walks on, a flock of birds settles on the church cross; we recall that when Jeanne was praying in her cell, Dreyer's long shot caught the scrawled graffito of a bird on the wall outside. At the stake, Jeanne is handed a cross and resigns herself to death. Yet she has not totally numbed herself to pain. This is a human martyr, one who is aware of both death's necessity and life's preciousness, who adds, "Don't let me suffer too long," whose actions send sympathetic reverberations through nature, and who, as she presses a cross to her bosom, glimpses a baby at its mother's breast. Jeanne's sacrifice is magnified when we realize that life still pulses strong in her.

The tension between Jeanne's resignation to death and her sense of life's value becomes even stronger in the succeeding shots. The executioner takes Jeanne's cross from her, lifts her up, straightens her against the stake, and ties the rope around her wrist; daringly, Dreyer keeps the camera framed on Jeanne, reducing the executioner chiefly to a pair of coolly businesslike hands. When the rope slips off Jeanne's wrist, her gesture of picking it up to give to the executioner is played entirely in a close-up following the hands: it becomes an abstract sign of utter resignation. As Jeanne is bound to the stake, the birds fly off the cross in the distance. The judges guiltily hurry into the church while the soldiers restrain the people. Massieu extends a crucifix to Jeanne on a pole. The birds soar overhead. Dreyer's camera tracks quickly across the smoking logs. Now Jeanne begins to fear death; quivering in fright and pain, she stifles her screams. This is what makes her finally more courageous than a totally complacent martyr would be; Jeanne has renounced the world, but she realizes what she is leaving; though she has chosen death, it terrifies her.

In the first shots of this sequence, the focus was almost entirely on Jeanne and the motifs (birds, crosses) that cluster around her. Now, gradually, Dreyer shifts to the crowd. Long tracking shots of weeping people, staring soldiers, and billowing smoke bring to the fore the political drama. When Warwick sees some people berate a soldier, he signals his men to be ready, and maces are dropped rhythmically to the waiting soldiers. In the meantime, Jeanne is writhing in agony as smoke obscures the cross Massieu extends. Close-ups juxtapose Jeanne's face, blurred by smoke and dirt, and (in subjective shots?) the crucifix's repeated movement to an upright position. Jeanne slumps over and cries, "Jesus!" Her spiritual drama is over.

But the political drama is reignited. The crowd now realizes that Jeanne is more than a military hero. A man turns from the stake to shout at Warwick: "You have burned a saint!" Immediately, the violence that has seethed steadily throughout the film erupts. The camera whips to the tower, Warwick rises and gestures angrily, and the army is unleashed on the town. What ensues is one of the most explosive scenes in silent cinema. The flailing maces of the soldiers pound ferociously into the crowd, knots of villagers and soldiers struggle, rocks smash the church windows. While employing elaborate low- and high-angle long shots, Dreyer also insists on close-ups, though the struggling figures all but burst out of the frame. Again and again, images of Jeanne's flaming body interrupt the action, like strains of a ghastly leitmotif. As quick tracking shots follow the fleeing crowd, Dreyer pauses to glimpse details: a woman running away clutching a lamb; a brief image of a child's feet as they race across the cobblestones to stop abruptly by the body of his mother, and—perhaps most eloquent of all—the hooded, enigmatic figure of Massieu wreathed in smoke and clutching a crucifix, as if numbed by the carnage around him. From the tower, soldiers fling spears into the crowd; on the ground, a cannon is leveled at the people and fired. Slowly the soldiers beat the crowd back across the drawbridge and the bridge is raised, cutting the people off from the castle. It is possible to criticize this sequence for excessive length (over sixty shots) and stylistic bravado (some somersaulting camera work), but this most visual of films demands a dynamically visual climax. The film has already pushed the techniques of close-up, crosscutting, and subjective camera work to extremes; what is required is a crescendo of great optical and rhythmic intensity. Scarcely a drop of blood is seen, but by cutting, camera movement, and the flow and collision of movement and images, this scene creates an impression of violence bursting all bounds. Thematically, the soldiers' slaying of children and mothers contrasts with the earlier images of the sucking baby, of the old woman giving Jeanne water, and of Jeanne's pressing the cross to her breast; by such a cluster of images, the army's brutality is presented as a monstrous attack not just on innocent people but on the life-principle itself. Not only, then, does this shattering violence climax the film's action at the political level, but its fury shows that the forces of death still rule the world Jeanne leaves.

The bleakness of this conclusion is not Dreyer's final word, however. Now, as decisively as a coda in a musical work, the thematic and formal progress of the film is completed by a single rich image which restates the tension of spiritual deliverance and political repression. The last shot frames the burning stake in the foreground, the stake which the English and the clergy saw as the ultimate solution to the political threat Jeanne posed—and a cross in the distance, the cross to which at moments of greatest pain Jeanne turned for consolation and, eventually, redemption. The result is a complex mixture of despair and affirmation.

Thus the developing visual tension of reality and abstraction has been accompanied by a developing dramatic tension between this world and another world; the way stylistic abstraction allows the film to be "not merely visual but spiritual" reflects Jeanne's decision to define herself not by an earthly mission but by her visionary commitment. Both stylistically and thematically, *La Passion de Jeanne d'Arc* is a transcendent film. "I wanted," Dreyer explained, "to interpret a hymn to the triumph of the soul over life."[7]

summary critique

La Passion de Jeanne d'Arc is not only aesthetically rich but historically significant. Widely and vigorously praised on its first appearance, it has since been regarded as outstandingly important: the 1958 Brussels critics' poll voted it one of the twelve best films ever made, and a 1972 *Sight and Sound* poll of critics from around the world reaffirmed the verdict. Yet such approval has been neither unanimous nor unqualified. Reactions proceeding from spleen or dogma—such as the Surrealist Jacques Brunius' condemnation of *Jeanne* as "one of the most *stinking* films I've ever seen"[1]—lie outside rational discussion, but more serious objections to the film demand consideration. Moreover, *La Passion de Jeanne d'Arc* is so utterly idiosyncratic that both attackers and defenders must wheel out their big artillery—their basic assumptions about film aesthetics and film history. Behind one's immediate response to the film loom large issues: in what sense film is an art; what constitutes the "essence" of cinema; the varieties of silent film style; sound film vs. silent film; and the ways in which film can render spiritual states. Whether one likes or dislikes *Jeanne d'Arc,* it is an important film because one who cares about cinema cannot ignore the questions it raises.

In retrospect, we can see that *La Passion de Jeanne d'Arc* was a crucial film in changing people's attitudes about cinema, particularly because of its decisive demonstration that film could be an art in its own right. Many observers immediately realized that *Jeanne d'Arc*'s sustained emotional crescendo had no equal in previous moviemaking. "As a film work of art," noted Mordaunt Hall in *The New York Times,* "this takes precedence over anything that has so far been produced. It makes worthy pictures of the past look like tinsel shams."[2] As a result, *Jeanne d'Arc* seemed to demand comparison not with ordinary films but with works in what were generally still regarded as the *real* arts. Abel Gance considered the film "worthy of the great sculptors of the Middle Ages,"[3] and Richard Watts saw it as "an amazing transcription of medieval art and the medieval devotional spirit."[4] The film's unprecedented stylistic rigor, the elevation of its subject, the impeccable credentials of its cast, and its refusal to cater to popular conceptions of entertainment constituted a daring bid for consideration as a full-fledged art work. For better or worse, *Jeanne d'Arc* (like *Caligari, Potemkin,* and, in later decades, *The Seventh Seal* and *L'Avventura*) convinced many viewers that the cinema could be intellectually respectable.

But the argument for the artistic status of film did not hinge wholly on the cinema's affinities with other arts. At the same time, much of the important current theoretical discussion maintained that the cinema possessed at least two expressive resources which did not exist in any other art form: editing and close-ups. By editing, one could construct "purely filmic" time and space; by close-ups one could penetrate the human face and lift objects to the status of symbols. Therefore, the argument runs, film is uniquely equipped to remake reality; the director need not passively register the world, he can create a world of his own—as the painter, the dramatist, or the poet can. *La Passion de Jeanne d'Arc,* for obvious reasons, was often summoned to support this position. Harry Alan Potamkin, for instance, hailed Dreyer's film as "the vindication of the major cinema devices."[5] Béla Balázs celebrated the film for its creation of a new temporal–spatial dramaturgy and the relentless close-ups which bared "the face of man."[6] Gance and Pabst, both of whom had pioneered creative editing and close-ups, praised the film highly.[7] And Werner Klinger explicated the film's form and style purely by the psychological effects of shot juxtaposition and camera angle.[8]

Yet the aestheticians of the silent film were by no means in unanimous agreement about *Jeanne*'s cinematic properties. No doubt Dreyer had used close-ups and cutting, but in an idiosyncratic way that could be traced to no contemporary style. For some observers, particularly in the Soviet camp, the film's scrupulous compositions and unique editing made it static. "Very interesting and beautiful," remarked Eisenstein of *Jeanne,* "but not a film. Rather a series of wonderful photographs."[9] What could make *Jeanne* "not a film"? Paul Rotha, a fervent admirer of Eisenstein, offered the most detailed explanation:

> The very beauty of the individual visual images destroyed the *filmic* value of the production. . . . This was in direct opposition to the central aim of the cinema, in which each individual image is inconsequential in itself, being but a part of the whole vibrating pattern. In Dreyer's beautiful film the visual image was employed to its fullest possible extent, but employed graphically and not filmically.[10]

As I have argued elsewhere, Rotha is judging Dreyer's film by Eisenstein's principle of montage of attractions, wherein the fact of juxtaposition by conflict makes the meaning of a sequence of shots greater than the sum of the separate meaning of each shot.[11] Actually, at many points in the film Dreyer does follow Eisenstein's model of shot-conflict: there are graphic conflicts (the small Jeanne versus the gross d'Estivet), dynamic conflicts (the clash of the still, staring Jeanne and the whirling torture wheel), and ideological conflicts (the cuts from the flaming stake to the enraged soldiers). But on the whole, Eisenstein and Rotha are correct in seeing that Dreyer's editing is essentially different from Eisenstein's. The question is whether this is bad or "unfilmic."

Rotha's error lies in assuming that only montage of attractions can achieve "the central aim of the cinema." Also, it is irresponsible to damn Dreyer's style without investigating its relation to the theme and form of the film as a whole, as at least one theorist of the time realized. In a sensitive essay, "Dreyer,

Léger, and Montage," Kirk Bond argues that while *La Passion de Jeanne d'Arc* bridges the gap between the intellectual cinema of Eisenstein and the sensuous cinema of Léger, the film remains essentially unique:

> [*Jeanne d'Arc*] is composed of fragments, but they are neither fragments of montage nor fragments of simple contrast. They are not really connected according to any accepted cinematic theory. Consequently it is only too easy to dismiss them merely as a series of beautiful photographs. This, however, will not do. Those beautiful pictures, however disconnected, are nevertheless welded together in a consummate continuity that transcends any technical objections.[12]

Some elements of this continuity—crosscutting, symbolic motifs, decor and lighting—were pointed out in the previous chapter; far from being merely a string of striking shots, the images constitute an expressive thematic and formal whole. Furthermore, despite *La Passion de Jeanne d'Arc*'s slight debt to Eisenstein, the film utilizes a basically different style. To dynamize a subject, Eisenstein frequently combines several shots taken from various angles (e.g., the statue at the beginning of *October*); Dreyer draws on this technique only in the torture sequence. Eisenstein often overlaps various conflicting shots of an object or action to stretch out time (the classic instance is the sailor's smashing of the plate in *Potemkin*), while *Jeanne d'Arc* makes virtually no use of this technique. Whereas Eisenstein's cutting frequently bursts his scenes open onto imaginary, metaphorical planes (the butchering of the bull in *Strike,* the stone lions in *Potemkin,* and the Napoleon statues in *October*), Dreyer sticks obstinately to the locale and dramatic time of his narrative, preferring to stylize decor and charge actions and objects *in* the scene with symbolic overtones. In fact, *Jeanne*'s cutting owes more to Griffith than to Eisenstein: as we've seen, crosscutting is essential to the film's form. In short, Eisenstein's and Dreyer's editing share a strong rhythmic drive, but whereas Eisenstein's style is expansive, Dreyer's tends to be compressive. Thus the film should not be found wanting simply because it fails to conform to the standards of one method of cinematic construction. Whatever is "essentially cinematic" will not be found by narrow *ad hoc* definitions.

Where, then, do *Jeanne d'Arc*'s stylistic affinities lie? Not the least remarkable dimension of this rich film is that while it strikes one as an absolutely original work, it nonetheless synthesizes many stylistic trends of the silent cinema. The abstract and occasionally distorted decors are the legacy of German Expressionist filmmaking (in which Hermann Warm, *Jeanne*'s set designer, was a prime figure). The subtlety of the acting, however, has none of the stylization of the Expressionist cinema and instead recalls the painstaking performances in Griffith and Sjöström. Likewise, the film's rhythmic cutting and typage owe something to the Soviet school, but, as suggested above, Dreyer's film does not rely on intellectual or metaphoric montage. A touch of Murnau is visible in Dreyer's use of the moving camera, while *Jeanne*'s slow tempo and intense concentration of time and locale suggest the influence of the German *kammerspiel* film, the principles of which had already entered Dreyer's work in *Mikael* and *The Master of the House*. Perhaps most influential of all was the French Impressionist style. Between 1919 and 1925, Gance, Epstein, and L'Herbier had experimented with quick cutting (e.g., the locomotive in Gance's *La Roue*) and subjective camerawork (e.g., Epstein's *Coeur Fidèle* and L'Herbier's *El Dorado* and *L'Argent*). In early 1926, Dreyer visited Gance during the shooting of *Napoleon,* glimpsed an actor filming first-person shots, and was reminded of similar effects in Dupont's *Variety*.[13] Thus it is no accident that in *Jeanne d'Arc* Dreyer turned, for the first time, to Impressionistic montage and subjective camerawork. In the context of film history, then, *La Passion de Jeanne d'Arc* becomes significant as a summation of many major film styles of the silent era.

A summation, some historians would add, that was also a

swan song. Experiments with sound-synchronized motion pictures had been conducted almost since the invention of cinema, but sound-on-film was not shown to be technically feasible until around 1927—the very year of *Jeanne d'Arc*'s production. Dreyer's film was caught in the squeeze of history: if *Jeanne* had appeared a year earlier, it would have slipped comfortably into the great silent film tradition; two years later, it would probably have been a sound film. The very title of one American review—"A Dying Art Offers a Masterpiece"—suggests how archaic the film must have looked in 1928. Moreover, *Jeanne d'Arc* could not tell its story through action alone; the very situation of Jeanne's trial demanded plenty of dialogue titles. Hence the film seemed a freakish mixture, at once a vindication of a dead art and a premature announcement of a future one. "Dreyer seems to have pushed the silent cinema to the very edge of its limitations," writes Arthur Knight. "It could go no further in baring the soul [sic] of its characters; already it was straining toward the added fluency of sound, the added levels of self-revelation possible in speech."[14] A French critic concisely summed up the paradox many people see in *Jeanne d'Arc:* "It is at once the last silent film and the first sound film."[15]

Undoubtedly, for many viewers today, the film's silence and its numerous dialogue titles are at best distractions and more often grave faults. Yet apart from the accident of historical timing, there is something to be said for *Jeanne*'s lack of sound. In the first place, there is the unique suspense which Parker Tyler has pointed out: "Visibly working lips invest the action with a special drama: we must wait for the next subtitle as if we heard the inquisitor's question and Joan's reply through some irksome time interval."[16] Furthermore, silence and titles are effective distancing devices, removing Jeanne's story still further from our world and contributing to the abstraction of the film as a whole. Nonetheless, the intrinsic appropriateness of *Jeanne*'s silence does not minimize the importance of the questions it raises about the different stylistic demands of silent and sound film.

Despite its ambiguous position in the filmmaking of the time, the long-range historical significance of *La Passion de Jeanne d'Arc* is clear. The film stands in solitary grandeur on the horizon of film history. The reason is apparent: *Jeanne d'Arc* closes off a set of stylistic possibilities; one cannot proceed further in this direction in this way than Dreyer has. As early as 1928, Evelyn Gerstein prophetically noted: "This is a cinema masterpiece . . . but a masterpiece that will probably be without issue."[17] One can trace small debts to *Jeanne d'Arc* in some recent works: the harsh close-ups of faces against white walls in East European films like Jancso's *Round Up* (1969) and Jires' *Joke* (1969); Nana's famous visit to the cinema in *Vivre Sa Vie* (1962), by means of which Godard confers on his prostitute the suffering of a saint; and, perhaps most explicitly, the style and subject of Jerzy Kawalerowicz's *Mother Joan of the Angels* (1961), which examines the link of holy passion to frustrated sexuality. But on the whole, *La Passion de Jeanne d'Arc* has had no imitators, no sequels, and little determinable influence. Even Bresson's *Procès de Jeanne d'Arc* (1961) is markedly different from Dreyer's film, and the question of influence is settled not only by the onscreen evidence but also by Bresson's contemptuous disclaimer: "I understand that in its time this film made a small revolution, but now I never watch it, since all its buffoonish actors and their frightful grimaces make me want to flee."[18] *Jeanne d'Arc*'s uniqueness makes it typical of most of Dreyer's output, which remains unimitated; as Dreyer once accurately observed, "I have no disciples."[19]

Paradoxically, though, the very isolation that makes the film a historical dead end gives it an absolute aesthetic autonomy. The abstraction and stylization which seals off *La Passion de Jeanne d'Arc* from much film history since 1928 also makes it easier for us to watch today. There are some silent films whose virtues need defending before a contemporary audience: what seem to us the excesses of *Way Down East* or *Metropolis* or *Greed* must be seen as conventions of the period or style. But certain silent films, by sheer creative force, transcend their historical context and impose their will on the audience as direct, immediate artistic experience. Their identities belong less to a time than to unique creative visions. Like *The Cabinet of Dr. Caligari, Nosferatu,* and *Potemkin, La Passion de Jeanne d'Arc* requires no apology: its aesthetic power is timeless.

In the longer view, it is this uncompromising authority which gives *La Passion de Jeanne d'Arc* its lasting importance. The film is, in the first place, a great work of religious art—not in any narrowly doctrinal sense but in the sense that it depicts, as a vital possibility, man's transcendence of material limitations in search of spiritual order. Jeanne's overpowering faith superbly incarnates the human need to believe in a higher moral realm than one can objectively ascertain. Not only does the drama set Jeanne's transcendent faith against the transitory demands of this world, but the film's very style and form *embody* religious experience. It's one thing for a director to make his characters talk about religious faith (e.g., Bergman's handling of Antonius Blok's crisis of belief in *The Seventh Seal*); it's quite another to present concretely, in the very texture of the film experience, such a dynamic mixture of awe, frenzy, stubbornness, contemplation, and resignation that we feel engaged in the process of achieving faith. Thus Henri Agel can without overstatement compare the image of Jeanne's face in Dreyer's film with the galvanizing touch that God bestows on man in Michelangelo's Sistine ceiling.[20] Both artists have succeeded in transforming the diffuse, elusive shimmer of religious ecstasy into the purified, intense luminescence of aesthetic experience.

Yet the other-worldly dimension of *La Passion de Jeanne d'Arc* should not seduce our feet too far off the ground, for the film's ultimate center of gravity is humanity. Despite all its stylization, the film escapes the trap of Expressionism by its respect for vital spontaneity. The time and space are never so abstract, the drama never so spiritual, that we forget the concrete physical immediacy of this world. "In this drama-through-the-microscope," writes André Bazin, "the whole of nature palpitates beneath every pore."[21] The religious dilemma of *Jeanne d'Arc* is presented as a human one: Jeanne's quest for the eternal and the absolute leads her over a terrain that is painfully of this world. Faith is not easy (e.g., Jeanne's internal struggle) and requires great courage (e.g., her defiance of torture). Most of all, faith requires an ultimate resignation, a willingness to define oneself utterly by the spiritual order one envisions. Jeanne's recantation in the face of death is a denial of her true self; her acceptance of martyrdom constitutes self-recognition. Jeanne's God may not exist—indeed, the final slaughter of the innocents casts grave doubt on the presence of a beneficent God. But whether Jeanne's last cry of "Jesus!" echoes across an empty cosmos or not, the human purpose of her mission has been accomplished. She has completely realized herself as an individual, and for me this assertion of one person's essential identity constitutes the greatest significance of the film.

More important, then, than the theoretical, aesthetic, and historical questions raised by *La Passion de Jeanne d'Arc* are the human ones. True, Dreyer inevitably neglects certain aspects of Jeanne which interest other artists: his film lacks the lyricism and humor of Honegger's oratorio, the sabrelike wit of Shaw's play, the sardonic bitterness of Brecht's drama. But Dreyer's film has a unique virtue. Of all the Jeannes in twentieth century art, none embodies more perfectly the possibility of achieving integrity by a humble but tenacious commitment to a transcendent ideal. From the zeal of the historical Jeanne d'Arc, Carl Dreyer's holy seriousness has wrought an enduring image of one way to become totally human.

a Dreyer filmography
bibliography
rental sources
notes

a Dreyer filmography

Films are listed in chronological order of production; dates are those of initial release.

Praesidenten (*The President*). 1920. Nordisk Films, Copenhagen.

Blade af Satans Bog (*Leaves from Satan's Book*). 1921. Nordisk Films, Copenhagen.

Prästänkan (*The Parson's Widow*). 1920. Svensk Filmindustri, Stockholm.

Die Gezeichneten (*The Stigmatized Ones; Love One Another*). 1922. Primusfilm, Berlin.

Der Var Engang (*Once Upon a Time*). 1922. Sophus Madsen, Copenhagen.

Mikael. 1924. Decla-Bioscop for UFA, Berlin.

Du Skal Aere Din Hustru (*Thou Shalt Honor Thy Wife; The Master of the House*). 1925. Palladium Film, Copenhagen.

Glomdalsbruden (*The Bride of Glomdal*). 1926. Victoria-Film, Oslo.

La Passion de Jeanne d'Arc. 1928. Société Générale des Films, Paris.

Vampyr. 1932. Tobis-Klangfilm, Berlin.

Modrehjaelpen (*Good Mothers*). 1942. Mogens Skot-Hansen, Copenhagen. (Documentary short)

Vredens Dag (*Day of Wrath*). 1943. Palladium Film, Copenhagen.

Två Människor (*Two People*). 1945. Svensk Filmindustri, Stockholm.

Vandet På Landet (*Water from the Land*). 1946. Palladium Film, Copenhagen. (Documentary short)

Landsbykirken (*The Danish Village Church*). 1947. Preben Frank, Copenhagen. (Documentary short)

Kampen Mod Kraeften (*The Struggle Against Cancer*). 1947. Preben Frank, Copenhagen. (Documentary short)

De Naede Faergen (*They Caught the Ferry*). 1948. Dansk Kultur-film, Copenhagen. (Short)

Thorvaldsen. 1949. Preben Frank, Copenhagen. (Documentary short)

Storstrømsbroen (*Storstrom Bridge*). 1950. Preben Frank, Copenhagen. (Documentary short)

Ordet (*The Word*). 1954. Palladium Film, Copenhagen.

Et Slot i et Slot (*Castle Within a Castle*). 1954. Teknisk Film, Copenhagen. (Documentary short)

Gertrud. 1964. Palladium Film, Copenhagen.

For complete credits for these films, see *L'Avant-Scène du Cinéma* 100 (February 1970), 39–43.

bibliography

I. SCRIPTS AND SYNOPSES

Dreyer, Carl. *Four Screenplays.* Bloomington: Indiana University Press, 1970. Includes a pre-production script of *Jeanne d'Arc* and an introduction with some material never before published in English.

Dreyer, Carl. *La Passione di Giovanna d'Arco.* Milan: Domus, 1945. A small but packed picture book which provides a rough continuity outline of the film supplemented by many frame enlargements. Useful for studying the film's compositions.

II. ESSAYS AND BOOKS BY DREYER

"A Little on Film Style." *Cinema,* VI, 2 (Fall 1970), 8–15. One of Dreyer's major essays, chiefly about *Day of Wrath* but with implications for *Jeanne d'Arc.* Intriguing if occasionally overwrought annotations by Don Skoller.

"Écrits." *Cahiers du Cinéma* 124 (October 1961), 23–35; 127 (January 1962), 27–35; 133 (July 1962), 16–24; 134 (August 1962), 29–36. French translations of several important essays from *Om Filmen* (q.v.). See especially "La Mystique Realisée," *Cahiers du Cinéma* 124 (October 1961), 34–35, for material on *La Passion de Jeanne d'Arc.* Highly recommended.

"The Filmmaker and the Audience." In Hughes, Robert, ed., *Film: Book I,* New York: Grove, 1959, 42–45. Interesting anecdotes about Dreyer's problems with producers, particularly regarding the editing of *Jeanne d'Arc.*

Om Filmen. Copenhagen: Gyldendals, 1964. A collection of essays, reviews, occasional pieces, and interviews revealing Dreyer's views on filmmaking. Essential for a study of *Jeanne d'Arc* is the essay "Realiseret mystik," 30–31.

"Thoughts on My Craft." *Sight and Sound* (Winter 1955–56). Reprinted in MacCann, Richard Dyer, ed., *Film: A Montage of Theories,* New York: Dutton, 1966, 312–17. One of Dreyer's most important essays, testifying to the importance he placed on stylistic simplification and abstraction.

III. INTERVIEWS WITH DREYER

Delahaye, Michel. "Between Heaven and Hell: Interview with Carl Dreyer." *Cahiers du Cinéma in English* 4, 7–15. Reprinted as "Carl Dreyer" in Sarris, Andrew, ed., *Interviews with Film Directors,* New York: Avon, 1969, 140–63. The most valuable Dreyer interview available in English: a sympathetic, informed questioner and a responsive interviewee explore problems of film history, the relation of theatre to cinema, and Dreyer's recurring themes and styles.

Lerner, Carl. "My Way of Working Is in Relation to the Future."
   Film Comment, IV, 1 (Fall 1966), 62–67. Although devoted
   primarily to *Gertrud,* the interview touches on several points
   relating to *Jeanne d'Arc.*
Manvell, Roger. "Lunch with Carl Dreyer." *Penguin Film Review*
   3 (August 1947), 67. Précis of a conversation during which
   Dreyer discussed *Jeanne d'Arc* and *Day of Wrath.*
Sadoul, Georges. "Carl Dreyer Nous Dit: 'Le principal intérêt
   d'un homme: les autres hommes.' " *Les Lettres Français* 1060
   (24–30 December 1964),   8. A survey of Dreyer's career
   via questions from the emperor of film historians.
Winge, John H. "Interview with Dreyer." *Sight and Sound* (January 1950), 16–17. Dreyer briefly discusses *Jeanne d'Arc*'s
   production, especially Falconetti's performance.

IV. SECONDARY SOURCES: REVIEWS, ESSAYS, AND BOOKS

Agel, Henri, and Ayfre, Amédée. *Le Cinema et le Sacre.* Paris:
   Editions du Cerf, 1953, 21–26, 130–31. Intriguing essays on
   religion in the cinema, with much material indirectly appli-
   cable to all Dreyer's films.
Amengual, Barthélemy. "Fonction du Gros Plan et du Cadrage
   dans *La Passion de Jeanne d'Arc.*" *Etudes Cinématographiques* 53–56 (1967), 154–63. Helpful stylistic study.
Ayfre, Amédée. "Les Voix du Silence." *Conversion aux Images?*
   Paris: Editions du Cerf, 1964, 95–99. A somewhat forced
   attempt to see the film's silence as the silence of Jeanne's
   voices and ultimately "the silence of the soul."
Ayfre, Amédée. "L'Univers de Dreyer." *Le Cinéma et Sa Vérité.*
   Paris: Editions du Cerf, 1969, 173–80. A phenomenological
   analysis of Dreyer; valuable remarks on Dreyer's handling
   of time and space.
Balázs, Béla. *Theory of the Film.* New York: Dover, 1970. Little

explicit commentary on *Jeanne d'Arc* but representative of the silent film aesthetic which *Jeanne* summarizes.

Bazin, André. *What Is Cinema?* I. Trans. Hugh Gray. Berkeley: University of California Press, 1967. Many illuminating references to *Jeanne,* such as the remark that "the greater recourse Dreyer has exclusively to the human 'expression,' the more he has to reconvert it again into Nature" (109).

Bond, Kirk. "Léger, Dreyer, and Montage." *Creative Art* (October 1932), 135–38. One of the earliest and soundest examinations of Dreyer's departures from the avant-garde traditions of Léger and Eisenstein.

Bordwell, David. *Dreyer.* London: November Books, 1973. A survey of Dreyer's characteristic styles and themes, analyses of his films, and essays on historical aspects of his career.

Bost, Pierre. *La Passion et la Mort de Jeanne d'Arc. Collection le Cinéma Romanesque* 7. Paris: Gallimard, 1928. Includes rare essays by Valentine Hugo, Jean Cocteau, and others.

Bowser, Eileen. *The Films of Carl Dreyer.* New York: Museum of Modern Art, 1964. Sketchy but occasionally helpful pamphlet.

"Carl Th. Dreyer." *Cahiers du Cinéma* 207 (December 1968). An immensely important collection of material by Dreyer (journalism, letters, film reviews), critical essays on his work, an annotated filmography, and even a phonograph record of an interview.

Delteil, Joseph. *La Passion de Jeanne d'Arc.* Paris: Editions M.P. Trémois, 1927. Delteil's draft of the film: labored and sentimental, it makes an interesting contrast with Dreyer's version.

Dyssegaard, Sören, ed. *Carl Th. Dreyer: Danish Film Director.* Copenhagen: Ministry of Foreign Affairs, 1968. A commemorative collection of essays (including one by Renoir) and excerpts from the *Jesus* film script.

Exposition Universelle et Internationale de Bruxelles. *Confrontation des Meilleurs Films de Tous les Temps.* Brussels: Ciné-

mathèque de Belgique, 1958. Pages iv–1 to iv–27 contain
an essay on *Jeanne d'Arc*'s camerawork by Ebbe Neergaard,
four extracts from the trial transcript, and four excerpts from
Bost's book.

Herring, Robert. *"La Passion de Jeanne d'Arc."* London Mer-
cury, 18 (August 1928), 424–26. A terse description of the
film, sensitive to acting and visual nuance.

"Jeanne d'Arc à l'Écran." *Études Cinématographiques* 18–19
(1962). An admirable collection of essays on Jeanne in
literature and film.

Jeanne, René, and Ford, Charles. *Histoire Encyclopédique du
Cinéma,* II. Paris: S.E.D.E., 1952, 70–77. Summarizes and
quotes several documents of the 1925–28 period that place
Jeanne in historical context.

Kelman, Ken. "Dreyer." *Film Culture* 35 (Winter 1964–65),
1–10. Economical and perceptive, this is one of the finest
essays ever written on Dreyer's films.

Klinger, Werner. "Analytical Treatise on the Dreyer Film, 'The
Passion of Joan of Arc.' " *Experimental Cinema,* I, 1 (February 1930), 7–10. An analysis of Dreyer's use of rhythm
and "plastic material."

Knight, Arthur. *The Liveliest Art.* New York: Mentor, 1957, 98–
99. Succinct statement of the standard historical judgments
passed on *Jeanne d'Arc.*

Lo Duca. "Trilogie Mystique de Dreyer." *Cahiers du Cinéma* 9
(February 1952), 61–63. Discusses the circumstances behind
the production of *Jeanne d'Arc* and explains the purpose of
the commercial sonorization.

Manvell, Roger. *The Film and the Public.* Harmondsworth: Penguin Books, 1955, 55, 119–23. A brief but sound survey of
many issues, both historical and thematic, raised by the film.

Marker, Chris. *"La Passion de Jeanne d'Arc."* In Chevalier,
Jacques, ed., *Régards Neufs Sur le Cinéma* 8. Paris: Seuil,

1953, 257–61. A master filmmaker analyzes Dreyer's use of time and the theme of the Devil in *Jeanne d'Arc*.

Milne, Tom. *The Cinema of Carl Dreyer*. London: Tantivy Press, 1971, 92–107. Offers a dissenting judgment on the efficacy of the film's style and some thoughtful remarks on the theme. The book as a whole constitutes a helpful introduction to Dreyer's *oeuvre*.

Moore, Paul. "The Tyrannical Dane." *Theatre Arts* (April 1951), 35–38. Lively article tracing Dreyer's career to 1950.

Moussinac, Léon. *L'Âge Ingrat du Cinéma*. Paris: Editions Français Réunis, 1967, 284–88. Sensitive review containing important historical material.

Neergaard, Ebbe. *Carl Theodor Dreyer: A Film Director's Work*. Trans. Marianne Helwig. London: BFI New Index Series 1, 1950. The standard study of Dreyer by a sympathetic friend and an acute critic. Much background material on *Jeanne d'Arc*. Highly recommended.

Neergaard, Ebbe. *The Story of Danish Film*. Copenhagen: The Danish Institute, 1962. Containing little about Dreyer and spoiled by maddening chronological gaps, this is nevertheless the only authoritative history of Danish cinema.

Parrain, Philippe. "Dreyer: Cadres et Mouvements." *Études Cinématographiques* 53–56 (1967), 1–151. A painstaking, exhaustive analysis of Dreyer's visual style.

"La Passion de Jeanne d'Arc." *L'Avant-Scène du Cinéma* 100 (February 1970), 44–54. Reprints much primary source material on *Jeanne d'Arc*.

Pernoud, Regine. *Joan of Arc*. New York: Grove, 1961.

———. *Joan of Arc by Herself and Her Witnesses*. New York: Stein and Day, 1966.

Two excellent studies of the historical Jeanne, the first a general consideration and summary, the second a detailed chronology with many excerpts from the trial transcript.

78   *Filmguide to La Passion de Jeanne d'Arc*

Perrin, Claude. *Carl Th. Dreyer.* Paris: Seghers, 1969. A helpful essay on recurring themes in Dreyer's work, supplemented by excerpts from critics' essays and an excellent bibliography.
Potamkin, Harry Alan. *"The Passion of Joan of Arc."* In Jacobs, Lewis, ed., *The Emergence of Film Art.* New York: Hopkinson and Blake, 1969, 118–21. Dithyrambic review, praising Falconetti highly.
Rotha, Paul. *The Film Till Now.* London: Vision Press, 1963, 301–07. Most coherent statement of the but-it-isn't-a-film position on *Jeanne d'Arc.*
Sadoul, Georges. *Le Cinéma Français.* Paris: Flammarion, 1962. Good background on the contemporary filmmaking situation surrounding *Jeanne d'Arc.*
Schrader, Paul. *Transcendental Style in Film: Ozu, Bresson, Dreyer.* Berkeley: University of California Press, 1972, 111–47. Interesting if sometimes inaccurate treatment of Dreyer's work as agony-torn Protestant art.
Sémolué, Jean. *Dreyer.* Paris: Editions Universitaires, 1962. A comprehensive study of Dreyer's work. Highly recommended.
Sémolué, Jean. *Carl Th. Dreyer. Anthologie du Cinéma* 53 (March 1970). A rapid overview of Dreyer's career; brief but penetrating discussion of *Jeanne d'Arc.*
Sémolué, Jean. "Douleur, Noblesse Unique." *Études Cinématographiques* 10–11 (Autumn 1961), 150–61. Analysis of themes of trial, torture, and sacrifice in Dreyer's work.
Sémolué, Jean. "Passion et Procès (De Dreyer à Bresson)." *Études Cinématographiques* 18–19 (Autumn 1962), 98–107. A close comparison of the two directors' conceptions of the heroine.
Trolle, Borge. "The World of Carl Dreyer." *Sight and Sound,* 25, 3 (Winter 1955–56), 123–27. A study of Dreyer's relation to Stanislavsky and to a Protestant-based conflict "between the death-instinct of the male and the life-affirmation of the female" (126).
Tyler, Parker. *Classics of the Foreign Film.* New York: Bonanza,

1962, 42–47. Brief but perceptive remarks on the film's style and theme.

Vincent, Carl. "Carl-Theodor Dreyer e la sua opera." "Filmografia ragionata." *Bianco e Nero,* 10, 10 (October 1949), 14–30. Contains much valuable material obtained by correspondence with Dreyer.

Watts, Richard, Jr. "A Dying Art Offers a Masterpiece." In Jacobs, Lewis, ed. *Introduction to the Art of the Movies.* New York: Noonday Press, 1960, 130–33. A sensitive contemporary response, applauding *Jeanne d'Arc*'s rejection of sound.

rental sources

16mm prints of the definitive Cinémathèque Française version of *La Passion de Jeanne d'Arc* may be rented from the Museum of Modern Art Film Library, 11 West 53rd Street, New York, New York 10019. The 1952 Gaumont sonorization is available from CCM Films, 34 MacQuesten Parkway South, Mount Vernon, New York 10550. The former version is preferable; the Gaumont reedition has replaced many inter-titles with subtitles, added titles filmed against stained-glass windows, and added a sound track of which Dreyer did not approve. Whichever version is rented, the film should be projected without sound at silent speed to respect Dreyer's intended tempo. *La Passion de Jeanne d'Arc* is one silent film that doesn't suffer by being shown without music.

notes

CHAPTER 3:   *The Director*

1. Bernard Shaw, Preface to *Saint Joan* (Baltimore, 1968), 25.
2. Carl Dreyer, "Idées Nouvelles dans le Cinéma," *Cahiers du Cinéma* 124 (October 1961), 28. Translated from Carl Dreyer, "Nye ideer i filmen," *Om Filmen* (Copenhagen, 1964), 20.
3. Dreyer, "Idées Nouvelles dans le Cinéma," 27.
4. Carl Dreyer, "Ma Seule Grande Passion," *Cahiers du Cinéma* 134 (August 1962), 29. Translated from Dreyer, "Min eneste store lidenskab," *Om Filmen*, 80.
5. Carl Vincent, "Carl-Theodor Dreyer e la sua opera," *Bianco e Nero* X, 10 (October 1949), 15.
6. Carl Dreyer, "Le Cinéma Suedois," *Cahiers du Cinéma* 124 (October 1961), 24. Translated from Carl Dreyer, "Svensk film," *Om Filmen*, 15–16.
7. Quoted in Ole Storm, Introduction, Carl Dreyer, *Four Screenplays* (Bloomington, 1970), 12. Translated from Carl Dreyer, "Filmsteknik og drejebøger," *Om Filmen*, 58–59.
8. Preben Thomsen, "Working with Dreyer," *Carl Th. Dreyer: Danish Film Director,* ed. Sören Dyssegaard (Copenhagen, 1968), 15.
9. Carl Dreyer, "Thoughts on My Craft," *Film: A Montage of Theories,* ed. Richard Dyer MacCann (New York, 1966), 315.
10. Quoted in Michel Delahaye, "Carl Dreyer," in *Interviews with Film Directors,* ed. Andrew Sarris (New York, 1969), 148.
11. Amédée Ayfre, "L'Univers de Dreyer," *Le Cinéma et sa Vérité* (Paris, 1969), 176.
12. Dreyer, "Ma Seule Grande Passion," 31.

CHAPTER 4:   *The Production*

1. Unless otherwise noted, material on the production of *La Passion de Jeanne d'Arc* has been taken from: Anonymous, *"La Passion de Jeanne d'Arc," L'Avant-Scène du Cinéma* 100 (February 1970), 44–54; Hermann Warm, "Laudatio" (undated), an unpublished manuscript; and Ebbe Neergaard, *Carl Dreyer: A Film Director's Work,* trans. Marianne Helwig (London, 1950), 19–26.
2. Quoted in Delahaye, 145.

3. Ibid., 155.
4. *La Passion de Jeanne d'Arc* (Paris, 1927). For excerpts from this text, see *L'Avant-Scène du Cinéma,* 47–48.
5. Quoted in Anonymous, "She Brushed Past Glory," *Pageant* (December 1962) [reprint, no page cited].
6. Quoted in Delahaye, 143.
7. Léon Moussinac, "Panoramique II," *L'Âge Ingrat du Cinéma* (Paris, 1967), 284.
8. Marcel Martin, *Le Langage Cinématographique* (Paris, 1967) 58.
9. Carl Dreyer, "La Mystique Realisée," *Cahiers du Cinéma* 124 (October 1961), 35. Translated from Carl Dreyer, "Realiseret Mystik," *Om Filmen,* 31.
10. Warm, "Laudatio," 3.
11. Quoted in Georges Sadoul, *Dictionnaire des Films* (Paris, 1965), 122.
12. Quoted in *L'Avant-Scène du Cinéma,* 47.
13. Quoted in Georges Sadoul, "Carl Dreyer Nous Dit . . . ," *Les Lettres Francais* 1060 (December 24–30, 1964), 8.
14. Quoted in Delahaye, 142.
15. Dreyer, "Thoughts on My Craft," 317.
16. Quoted in *L'Avant-Scène du Cinéma,* 47.
17. Carl Vincent, "Filmografia ragionata," *Bianco e Nero,* X, 10 (October 1949), 27.
18. Moussinac, 284n.
19. See Mordaunt Hall, "Poignant French Film," *New York Times* (31 March 1929), sec. VIII, 7.
20. Quoted in Exposition Universelle et Internationale de Bruxelles, *Confrontation des Meilleurs Films de Tous les Temps* (Brussels, 1958), iv–25.
21. Antonin Artaud, *Oeuvres Complètes,* III (Paris, 1961), 108.
22. Quoted in Sadoul, "Carl Dreyer Nous Dit . . . ," 8.
23. Henrik Stangerup, *"Gertrud,"* *Cahiers du Cinéma* 207 (December 1968), 74.

CHAPTER 5: *Analysis*

1. Dreyer, "Thoughts on My Craft," 315.
2. For a detailed comparison of Dreyer's Jeanne to the historical Jeanne, see Jean Sémolué, *Dreyer* (Paris, 1962), 55–57.
3. Siegfried Kracauer, *Theory of Film* (New York, 1960), 80.

4. André Bazin, *What Is Cinema?*, I, trans. Hugh Gray (Berkeley, 1967), 109.
5. Jean Mitry, *Esthétique et Psychologie du Cinéma*, I (Paris, 1963), 359.
6. Sémolué, 61.
7. Dreyer, "La Mystique Realisée," 35.

CHAPTER 6:   *Summary Critique*

1. Quoted in J.H. Matthews, *Surrealism and Film* (Ann Arbor, 1971), 17.
2. Mordaunt Hall, "Poignant French Film," 7.
3. Quoted in program note, American premiere, Little Carnegie Playhouse, 28 March 1929.
4. Richard Watts, "A Dying Art Offers a Masterpiece," *New York Herald Tribune* (31 March 1929), reprinted in *Introduction to the Art of the Movies*, ed. Lewis Jacobs (New York, 1960), 133.
5. Harry Alan Potamkin, *The National Board of Review* (1929), reprinted in *The Emergence of Film Art*, ed. Lewis Jacobs (New York, 1969), 118.
6. Béla Balázs, *Theory of the Film* (New York, 1970), 60–88.
7. Gance, program note for premiere. See also Hilda Doolittle, "An Appreciation," *Close-Up* IV, 3 (March 1929), 59.
8. Werner Klinger, "Analytical Treatise on the Dreyer Film, 'The Passion of Joan of Arc,'" *Experimental Cinema* I, 1 (February 1930), 7–10.
9. Quoted in Anonymous, "M. [sic] Eisenstein's Next Film," *New York Times* (16 February 1930), sec. IX, 6.
10. Paul Rotha, *The Film Till Now* (London, 1963), 305.
11. See S.M. Eisenstein, *Film Form* (New York, 1963), 28–63.
12. *Creative Art* (October 1932), 138.
13. Carl Dreyer, "Le Cinéma Francais," *Cahiers du Cinéma* 124 (October 1961), 32–34. Translated from Carl Dreyer, "Fransk film," *Om Filmen*, 28–29.
14. Arthur Knight, *The Liveliest Art* (New York, 1957), 98.
15. Quoted in Georges Sadoul, "Carl Dreyer Nous Dit . . . ," 8.
16. Parker Tyler, *Classics of the Foreign Film* (New York, 1962), 44.
17. Evelyn Gerstein, "Joan of Arc," *New Republic*, LVIII, 749 (10 April 1929), 22.
18. Quoted in *L'Avant-Scène du Cinéma*, 52. For a detailed compari-

son of Dreyer's film with Bresson's, see Jean Sémolué, "Passion et Procès," *Études Cinématographiques* 18–19 (Autumn 1962), 98–107.

19. Quoted in Stanley Kauffmann, *A World on Film* (New York, 1966), 404.

20. Henri Agel and Amédée Ayfre, *Le Cinéma et le Sacre* (Paris, 1953), 23.

21. Bazin, 110.